CW01249988

THE CONCISE DICTIONARY OF

GREAT SCOTS

BETTY KIRKPATRICK

Crombie Jardine
PUBLISHING LIMITED

Unit 17, 196 Rose Street, Edinburgh EH2 4AT
www.crombiejardine.com

Published by Crombie Jardine Publishing Limited
First edition, 2005

Copyright © 2005,
Crombie Jardine Publishing Limited

All rights are reserved. No part of this publication may be reproduced, stored in a retrieval system, or transmitted, in any form or by any means, electronic, mechanical, photocopying, recording or otherwise, without the prior written permission of the publisher.

ISBN 1-905102-31-3

Written by Betty Kirkpatrick
Designed by www.glensaville.com
Printed & bound in the United Kingdom by
William Clowes Ltd, Beccles, Suffolk

Introduction

In terms of landmass and population Scotland is a small country but, throughout the centuries, the Scots have regularly punched above their weight when it comes to providing people who have made an impact on the world.

The Scottish contribution to the world has encompassed many fields. Historically, people tend to think of the Scots as a nation of engineers and certainly the country has produced a good few of these. Thomas Telford, James Watt and John MacAdam are cases in point. However, the Scots have also demonstrated their talent and expertise in many other areas.

It is difficult to say which of the inventions in the world have been of greatest benefit to mankind, but medical advances are certainly among these and Scotland has produced many doctors and surgeons who have furthered medical knowledge. Among these is Alexander Fleming who discovered penicillin and made way for the extensive range of antibiotics that we have today. Before the discovery of penicillin a huge proportion of the population died of infections and diseases which are now curable.

But Scotland has not rested on its laurels and its doctors have continued to make a valuable contribution to medical advances. In particular, Ian Donald invented the first practical ultrasound scanner and developed its use in monitoring the development of the foetus in the womb. This has greatly relieved the anxiety levels of mothers-to-be during pregnancy.

Scots have not confined their talents to the world of science, though. They have also made a significant contribution to the arts. In the world of literature there are few names so famous in the world as that of the Scottish poet Robert Burns, and the work of Charles Rennie Mackintosh has had a major influence on designers throughout the world.

There has been something of a literary renaissance in modern Scotland and there is currently an exceptional number of Scottish writers producing successful works. Scots writers today, notably Ian Rankin, seem to be particularly good at crime fiction.

Scotland has given the world a whole range of famous people, from explorers such as Mungo Park, to football managers such as Jock Stein, and film actors like Sean Connery who has become something of a Scottish icon. Acting is another area which is enjoying a renaissance in Scotland today.

Obviously this is a small book. Its very size imposes restrictions on the number of people included and the information given about each. Obviously not all well-known Scots were admirable. As the title would suggest, for the most part, this book highlights commendable Scots and omits the criminals, such as serial killers. Apologies if your favourite Scot is missing. Still, there is enough here to whet your appetite.

Betty Kirkpatrick
Edinburgh
2005

GREAT SCOTS

A

Adam, Robert (1728-92) Architect, born in Kirkcaldy. He established the neoclassical style of architecture in Britain, examples of his fine work including buildings in Charlotte Square, Edinburgh, Register House, Edinburgh and Culzean Castle in Ayrshire.

Adamson, Robert (1821-48) Chemist and photographer, born in St Andrews. He formed a partnership with photographer **David Octavius Hill** to make photographic prints using the newly invented calotype process.

Aikman, William (1682-1731) Artist, born in Cairney, Forfarshire. One of the most prominent portrait painters of his generation, he is noted for his portrait of the poet **Allan Ramsay** (1722).

Aird, Ian (1905-62) Surgeon, born in Edinburgh. He carried out the first operation to separate Siamese twins in Britain, but is best known for developing kidney transplant surgery in the UK.

Alexander III (1241-86) King of Scotland. During his reign there was prosperity and peace with England. He acquired the Hebrides from Norway following the Battle of Largs (1263). His accidental death lead to a succession crisis.

Allan, David (1744-96) Artist, born in Alloa. He painted scenes from ordinary Scottish life, such as *The Highland Dance* (1780), and pioneered this style of painting in Scotland.

Allardyce, Captain Robert Barclay (1779-1854) Walker, born near Stonehaven. He is noted for his feat of walking 1,000 miles (1,609km) in 1,000 consecutive hours at Newmarket during June to July 1809.

Anderson, Arthur (1792-1868) Shipping magnate and philanthropist, born in Shetland. In 1840 he set up the P&O shipping line. He established the Anderson Education Institute in Lerwick (1862).

Anderson, Sir Robert Rowand (1834-1921) Architect, born in Edinburgh. He worked in many styles from gothic to classical. His buildings include the Edinburgh University Medical School (1874) and the Scottish National Portrait Gallery.

Anderson, Tom (1910-91) Born in Eshaness, Mainland Shetland. He did much to preserve the Shetland fiddle-playing technique and spread its influence. He taught **Aly Bain** and many others and collected and composed hundreds of tunes.

Andrew, St. Fisherman who, with his brother Simon Peter, became one of the disciples of Christ. He was adopted as the patron saint of Scotland, his feast day being November 30.

Annan, James Craig (1864-1946) Photographer, born in Hamilton. He studied the art of photogravure, a photographic etching process, in Vienna. He became a master of the technique and gained an international reputation.

Arrol, Sir William (1839-1913) Engineer and railway contractor, born in Houston in Renfrewshire. He was responsible for the Forth Railway Bridge (1890), the rebuilding of the Tay Railway Bridge (1889) and the Tower Bridge, London (1899).

Asquith, Margot (née **Tennant**) (1864-1945) Society hostess, wit and writer, wife of Prime Minister Herbert Asquith, born in Peebleshire. She was noted for her extravagant, flamboyant lifestyle and wrote two rather indiscreet autobiographies.

Atholl, Katherine, Duchess of (née **Ramsay**) (1874-1960) Conservative politician, born in Bamff, Perthshire. She was the first woman Conservative politician to be made a minister as Parliamentary Secretary to the Board of Trade (1924-29).

Atkinson, Kate (1951-) Writer, born in York. Her first novel *Behind the Scenes at the Museum* won the Whitbread Book of the Year (1995). Later works include *Emotionally Weird* (2000).

Ayton, Sir Robert (1570-1638) Courtier and poet, born near St Andrews. A courtier of James V and I, he wrote poems in Latin and English, possibly including a prototype of *Auld Lang Syne*.

B

Baillie, Dame Isobel (1885-1983) Soprano, born in Hawick. She began her professional singing career with the Halle Orchestra in Manchester and later sang for many of the world's most famous conductors.

Bain, Alexander (1818-1903) Philosopher and psychologist, born in Aberdeen. Among his most important works are *The Senses and the Intellect* (1855) and *Mental and Moral Science* (1868). He founded the journal *Mind* in 1876.

Bain, Aly (1946-) Musician, born in Lerwick, Shetland. He is a popular fiddle-player in the Scottish tradition. A founder member of the group the Boys of the Lough, he often plays with **Phil Cunningham**.

Baird, Dugald (1899-1986) Gynaecologist. He introduced cervical screening in Aberdeen in 1986. A supporter of free choice in abortion, he had a significant influence on the Abortion Act of 1967.

Baird, John Logie (1888-1946) Television pioneer, born in Helensburgh. In 1926 he gave the first demonstration of a television image. The BBC adopted his system in 1929 but in 1937 went over to a rival system made by Marconi-EMI.

Ballantyne, R(obert) M(ichael) (1825-94) Children's author, born in Edinburgh. He wrote *The Young Fur Traders* (1856), based on his experiences with the Hudson Bay Company, but his best-known novel is *Coral Island* (1858).

Banks, Iain (1954-) Novelist, born in Dunfermline. His first novel *The Wasp Factory* (1884), a study of insanity, achieved great acclaim. He also writes science fiction novels, such as *Consider Plebas* (1987) under the name **Iain M. Banks**.

Bannen, Iain (1928-99) Actor, born in Airdrie. Originally a stage actor, he appeared in many films, such as *Hope and Glory* (1987) and *Braveheart* (1995). His many TV roles included Dr Cameron in *Doctor Finlay's Casebook* (1993-96).

Barbour, John (c.1316-1395) Poet and churchman. Much of his poetry has been lost but his great poem *The Brus* about Robert the Bruce survives.

Barrie, Sir J(ames) M(atthew) (1860-1937) Novelist and dramatist, born in Kirriemuir. He wrote a number of rather sentimental novels and plays, several in the Kailyard tradition, but is best known for his ever-popular play *Peter Pan* (1904).

Bartholomew, John George (1860-1920) Cartographer, born in Edinburgh. The son of Edinburgh publisher **John Bartholomew** (1831-93), he joined the family firm and published atlases. He devised a system of indicating contours by colour.

Baxter, Jim (1939-2001) Football player, born in Fife. He played for Rangers (1960-64) and also for Nottingham Forest and Sunderland. Very popular with the fans, he was capped for Scotland 34 times.

Baxter, Stanley (1926-) Actor and comedian, born in Glasgow. He made many stage, radio and film appearances, but is perhaps best known for his television appearances, such as *The Stanley Baxter Show* (1968-71).

Bell, Alexander Graham (1847-92) Inventor, born in Edinburgh. In America he produced intelligible telephonic transmission and established the Bell Telephone Company in 1877. However, the US Congress in 2001 officially recognized Antonio Meucci as the inventor of the telephone.

Bell, Henry (1767-1830) Engineer, born in Linlithgow. He successfully introduced Europe's first passenger-carrying steamboat, launching the Comet (1812) which plied between Greenock and Glasgow.

Bell, Patrick (1799-1869) Inventor, born near Dundee. He invented the world's first practical reaping machine (1826-28). Some of his machines were sent to America which enabled Cyrus McCormick to improve on the design.

Bellany, John (1942-) Artist, born in Port Seton. He gained international fame with his large-scale, symbolic figurative paintings, often painted in bold colours.

His early works were influenced by his fishing background and German art.

Black, Joseph (1728-99) Chemist, born in Bordeaux, educated in Glasgow and Edinburgh. He discovered that there were gases other than air, particularly carbon dioxide, and evolved the theory of latent heat.

Blackadder, Elizabeth (1931-) Artist, born in Falkirk. The first Scottish woman to be elected to full membership of the Royal Scottish Academy (1972) and the Royal Academy (1976), she was appointed Queen's Limner in Scotland in 2001.

Blackie, John (1782-1874) Publisher. He established the firm of Blackie & Son in Glasgow in 1809. The firm went on to specialize in children's books and educational books before being bought out in 1993.

Blackwood, William (1776-1834) Publisher, born in Edinburgh. He founded *Blackwood's Magazine* (1817-1980) as a Tory rival to the Whig *Edinburgh Review*. The early issues of the magazine had as contributors several major writers such as **James Hogg**, and **John Buchan**.

Blair, Tony (Anthony) (1953-) Politician, born in Edinburgh. Elected to parliament in 1883, he succeeded **John Smith** as Leader of the Labour Party and introduced measures to modernize the party. He became Prime Minister in 1997.

Blind Harry (1470-92) Poet. He wrote *The Wallace*, a long heroic poem about William Wallace. The poem did much to establish Wallace as a heroic national figure, although it is not historically factual.

Blyth, Sir Chay (Charles) (1940-) Yachtsman, born in Hawick. In 1966 he rowed across the Atlantic with John Ridgeway and in 1971 he became the first person to sail solo non-stop round the world, westwards.

Boswell, James (1740-95) Writer. He accompanied Samuel Johnson on a tour of the Hebrides, described in *Journal of a Tour to the Hebrides* (1785) and published *A Life of Samuel Johnson* in 1791.

Bower, Walter (1385-1449) Historian, born in Haddington. Abbot of Inchcolm, he continued John of Fordun's *Chronica Genus Scotorum*. The result, *The Scotichronicon* (c.1440), is the first connected history of Scotland and valuable source material.

Boyd, William (1952-) Novelist, born in West Africa of Scottish parents. His novels include

The Ice Cream War (1982), *Brazzaville Beach* (1990), (1990), and *Any Human Heart* (2002).

Boyd Orr, John, Lord (1880-1971) Biologist, born near Kilmarnock. A pioneer of research into animal and human nutrition and the first director of the United Nations Food and Agricultural Organization, he won the Nobel Peace Prize in 1949.

Braid, James (1795-1860) Surgeon and hypnotist, born in Fife. A surgeon who specialized in club-foot operations, he pioneered what he called neurohypnosis, now called hypnosis.

Braid, James (1870-1950) Golfer, born in Earlsferry, Fife. Originally a joiner and a club-maker, he became a professional golfer in 1893 and won the Open Championship five times between 1901 and 1910.

Bremner, Billy (1942-97) Footballer, born in Stirling. He played for Leeds United (1959-76), being manager (1985-88). He was capped 54 times for Scotland. There is a statue of him at Elland Road, Leeds United's ground.

Bremner, Rory (1961-) Impressionist and comedian, born in Edinburgh. He began his career satirizing cricket commentators, but is best known for his impersonations of politicians.

Brewster, Sir David (1781-1868) Physicist, born in Jedburgh. He invented the kaleidoscope, conducted research into the polarization of light, and worked on improvements to the projection of light in lighthouses.

Bridie, James (1888-1951) Doctor and dramatist, born in Glasgow. His best-known play is *The Anatomist* (1931), about

Burke and Hare. He helped to found the Citizens' Theatre, Glasgow (1943).

Brisbane, Sir Thomas (1773-1860) Astronomer and soldier, born in Largs. When he was Governor of New South Wales (1821-25), he catalogued more than 7000 stars. Brisbane, capital of Queensland, is named for him.

Brown, George Douglas (1869-1902) Novelist, born in Ochiltree, Ayrshire. Using the pseudonym George Douglas, he wrote *The House with Green Shutters* (1901), whose realism contrasted sharply with the sentimentality of the Kailyard School.

Brown, George Mackay (1921-96) Poet and author, born in Stromness, Orkney. His work draws on the landscape, traditions and folklore of Orkney. His novel *Beside the Ocean of Time* (1994) was shortlisted for the Booker Prize.

Brown, Gordon (1951-) Politician, born in Kirkcaldy. Elected Labour MP for Dunfermline East (1983), he was tipped as potential party leader on the death of **John Smith**. He was appointed Chancellor of the Exchequer when Labour came to power in 1997.

Bruce, Sir David (1855-1931) Microbiologist, born in Australia of Scottish parents. He identified the tsetse fly as the source of sleeping sickness and discovered the bacteria brucella, the cause of brucellosis in cattle.

Bruce, James (1730-94) Explorer, born in Kinnaird, near Dundee. He travelled in Abyssinia and reached the source of the Blue Nile (1770), wrongly believing it to be the source of the Nile itself.

Bruce, Robert the *see* **Robert I**.

Bruce, William (1630-1710) Architect, born in Blairhall, near Dunfermline.

He introduced classical architecture to Scotland after 1660, rebuilt the Palace of Holyroodhouse in Edinburgh and designed part of Hopetoun House in West Lothian.

Bryden, Bill (1942-) Director and playwright, born in Greenock. Head of drama for BBC Scottish Television (1984-93), he wrote and directed *The Ship*, an epic play about the Glasgow shipbuilding industry (1990), during Glasgow's European year of Culture.

Buchan, John, 1st Baron Tweedsmuir (1875-1940) Author and politician, born in Perth. A prolific writer, he is best-known as the writer of spy thrillers such as *The Thirty-Nine Steps* (1915) and *Greenmantle* (1916).

Buchanan, Jack (1891-1957) Actor and entertainer. Originally a song-and-dance stage performer, he made his Broadway debut in 1924. He then appeared in a number of Hollywood films such as *Brewster's Millions* (1935).

Buchanan, Ken (1945-) Boxer, born in Edinburgh. He won the World Boxing Association lightweight championship in 1970, the first Briton to do so since 1917, and defended his title successfully twice in the USA.

Buick, David (1854-1929) Car manufacturer, born in Arbroath. Taken to America as a child, he built his first car in 1903 and formed the Buick Motor Company, taken over by the General Motors Corporation in 1908.

Burns, Sir George (1795-1890) Ship owner, born in Glasgow. He and his brother **James** developed steam navigation on the Clyde and he was one of the founders of the Cunard line.

Burns, Robert (1759-96) Poet, born in Alloway, near Ayr. Scotland's best known poet, he is also famous internationally. He wrote songs and poems in a number of genres and on many themes, using both Scots and English.

Burrell, William (1861-1958) Art collector. He made a gift of his huge collection of art works to the city of Glasgow (1944). This is on public show in Pollock Park.

Busby, Sir Matt (1909-94) Football manager, born in Bellshill, Lanarkshire. Many of his young team were killed in an air crash at Munich airport (1958) but he rebuilt the team and they won the European Cup (1968).

Byrne, John (1940-) Dramatist and stage designer, born in Paisley. As a stage dramatist he is noted for *The Slab Boys* (1978) which developed into a trilogy for television. He wrote the highly acclaimed *Tutti Frutti* (1987).

Byron, George Gordon, Lord (1788-1826) Poet, born in London but half-Scots by birth. One of the leading poets of his age, he is best known for *Don Juan* (1819-24). Scandal drove him to live abroad.

C

Cadell, Francis Campbell Boileau (1883-1937) Artist, born in Edinburgh. One of the Scottish Colourists, he is noted for his portraits, stylish interior scenes and paintings of Iona.

Cameron, Charles (1743-1812) Architect. At the invitation of the Empress Catherine the Great, he was the architect of several major buildings in St Petersburg, including Pavlovsk Palace.

Campbell, Colin (1679-1726) Architect, born in Morayshire. He was instrumental in the introduction of Palladianism into Britain. One of his best-known buildings is Burlington House in London (1718-19).

Campbell, Sir Colin, Lord Clyde (1792-1863) Soldier, born in Glasgow. He played a significant part in the British victory at Balaclava and he was the leading British commander during the Indian mutiny of 1857.

Campbell, Donald (1940-) Playwright and poet, born in Wick. One of the principal exponents of the new wave of theatre in the 1970s and 1980s, he wrote *The Jesuit* (1976) and *the Widows of Clyth* (1979).

Campbell, John Francis (1822-85) Folklorist, born in Islay. He collected considerable amounts of Gaelic literature and information on Gaelic customs and folklore. His works include *Tales of the West Highlands* (1860-62).

Campbell, Thomas (1777-1844) Poet, born in Glasgow. He is particularly remembered for his war poems such as *The Battle of the Baltic, Hohenlinden,* and *Ye Mariners of England.*

Campbell-Bannerman, Sir Henry (1836-1908) Politician, born in Glasgow. Elected MP for Stirling (1868), he became leader of the Liberal Party in 1899 and Prime Minister (1905), resigning in 1908 just before his death.

Carlyle, Jane Welsh (1801-66) Writer, born in Haddington. She married Thomas Carlyle (1926). Her letters and diaries, edited by her husband and published after her death in 1883, indicate her great writing talent.

Carlyle, Robert (1961-) Actor, born in Glasgow. He first came to prominence in the TV series *Hamish Macbeth*, being later noted for appearances in such films as *Trainspotting* (1996) and *The Full Monty* (1997).

Carlyle, Thomas (1795-1881) Writer, born in Ecclefechan in Dumfriesshire. Regarded as one of the most important writers of his age, he wrote *Sartor Resartus*, a work on social philosophy, and a six-volume history of Frederick the Great.

Carnegie, Andrew (1835-1919) Industrialist and philanthropist, born in Dunfermline. Emigrating to America, he made a large fortune from his iron and steel works and from railroads. His gifts and endowments in Britain and America exceeded £70 million.

Carson, Willie (1942-) Jockey, born in Stirling. In 1972 he was the first Scot to be champion jockey and has ridden 17 classic winners. He retired in 1996 after an accident.

Carswell, Catherine (1879-1946) Born in Glasgow. An important figure in Scottish women's writing, she wrote the novel *Open the Door* (1920) as well as biographies of DH Lawrence and Robert Burns.

Carswell, John (c.1525-72) Bishop, born in Kilmartin. Bishop of the Isles, he translated the

Book of Common Order into Gaelic (1567) and this was the earliest printed book in Gaelic.

Caskie, Donald (1902-83) Minister, born in Bowmore, Islay. As minister of the Scots Kirk in Paris, he assisted a great many people to escape from Nazi occupied France and described his experiences in *The Tartan Pimpernel* (1957).

Chalmers, James (1782-1853) Bookseller and inventor, born in Arbroath. He invented adhesive postage stamps and exhibited them publicly in 1834. His invention made Rowland Hill's Penny Postal service a practical proposition.

Chambers, Robert (1802-71) Publisher and writer, born in Peebles. With his brother **William** he started the publishing firm W&R Chambers. He was a prolific writer, his works including *The Traditions of Edinburgh* (1824).

Chambers, William (1800-83) Publisher and writer, born in Peebles. He started *Chambers Journal* (1832) and, with his brother **Robert**, set up the publishing firm W&R Chambers which became a major publisher of dictionaries and reference books.

Chapman, Walter (c.1473-c.1538) Printer. A wealthy merchant, he provided the funding for the establishment, in Edinburgh, of the first Scottish printing press (1507). His partner was **Andrew Myllar**.

Clark, Jim (1936-68) Racing driver, born in Kilmany, Fife. Twice world champion racing driver (1963, 1965), he held the record for Grand Prix victories when he was killed in a practice race in Germany.

Cleghorn, George (1716-94) Army surgeon. He discovered that quinine bark acted as a cure for malaria, a type of which was common in Britain at the time.

Clerk, Sir Dugald (1854-1932) Born in Glasgow, mechanical engineer. In 1881 he patented a gas engine working on the two-stroke principle, which became known as the Clerk Cycle.

Cochrane, Sir Ralph Alexander (1895-1977) Air chief marshal born in Springfield, Fife. He was responsible for planning the British bomber offensive against German industrial targets during World War II, including the famous Dambuster's Raid (1943).

Cockburn, Alison (1713-94) Poet born in Selkirkshire. A leading member of Edinburgh society, she is remembered for her version of the well-known lament *The Flowers o' the Forest* (1765).

Collins, William (1789-1853) Publisher, born in Eastwood, Renfrewshire. In 1819 he helped to set up a publishing business, producing school textbooks and religious works, including the Bible. The firm expanded and flourished under his descendants.

Coltrane, Robert (1950-) Actor, born in Rutherglen. He became known for the television series *Tutti Frutti* (1987) and *Cracker* (1993-96) and for films such as *Nuns on the Run* (1989). He played Hagrid in the *Harry Potter* films.

Columba St. (521-597) Abbot and missionary, born in Donegal. He established a monastery at Iona (563) which became the mother church of Celtic Christianity in Scotland. He did much to spread Christianity among the Picts.

Conan Doyle, Sir Arthur (1859-1930) Novelist, born in Edinburgh. He is best remembered for the exploits of his famous fictional detective Sherlock Holmes. *The Adventures of Sherlock Holmes* were first serialized in *Strand Magazine* (1891-93).

Conn, Stewart (1936-) Poet and dramatist, born in Glasgow. A BBC producer for many years, as a dramatist he was part of the theatrical revival of the 1970s and 1980s and wrote such plays as *The Burning* (1971).

Connery, Sir Sean (1930-) Actor, born in Edinburgh. He became an international star as James Bond in *Doctor No* (1962) and starred in several other Bond movies. More recent successes include *Indiana Jones and the Last Crusade* (1989).

Connolly, Billy (1942-) Comedian, born in Glasgow. A folk singer with a group known as The Humbledons, he became better known for his jokes and became a well-known stand-up comedian, known as the Big Yin, later becoming a film actor.

Constable, Archibald (1774-1827) Publisher, born in Carnbee, Fife. Publisher of the *Edinburgh Review* (1802), he was the publisher of leading writers including Walter Scott, and purchased the copyright of the *Encyclopaedia Britannica* (1812), but went bankrupt (1826).

Cook, Robin (1946-2005) Politician, born in Bellshill, Lanarkshire. Labour MP for Edinburgh Central (1874-83) and for Livingston (1983-2005), he resigned from the Cabinet (2003) in protest against Britain's involvement in the invasion of Iraq.

Corbett, Ronnie (1930-) Born in Edinburgh. Although appearing in several TV comedy shows, such as *Sorry* (1981), he is best known for his partnership with

Ronnie Barker in the popular, long-running 1970s TV series *The Two Ronnies*.

Corries, the Popular folk group formed by Roy Williamson (1936-90) and Ronnie Browne (1937-). They were especially noted for their rendition of *Flower of Scotland,* written by Roy Williamson and adopted as an unofficial Scottish national anthem.

Coulthard, David (1971-) Racing driver, born in Dumfries. He became a Formula 1 driver in 1994, when he was Scottish Sports Personality of the Year. He recorded six wins for the McLaren team between 1994 and 1999.

Cousin, David (1809-78) Architect, born in Edinburgh. He was involved in the replanning of much of Edinburgh's Old Town, such as Chambers Street and St Mary's Street, for the City Improvement Trust.

Craig, James (1744-95) Architect, born in Edinburgh. He was the architect responsible for designing the first phase of Edinburgh's New Town and for the building of Observatory House on Calton Hill in Edinburgh.

Cruickshank, Andrew (1907-88) Actor, born in Aberdeen. He made several stage and film appearances, but is best remembered for his TV role of the gruff Dr Cameron in *Dr Finlay's Casebook* (1962-71).

Cruickshank, Helen (1886-1975) Poet, born in Hillside, near Montrose. A writer of verse in both English and Scots, she was a prominent member of the literary circle which surrounded **Hugh MacDiarmid**.

Cullen, William (1710-90) Chemist and physician, born in Hamilton. He placed great emphasis on the importance of the nervous system in the causing of disease and he coined the word 'neurosis'.

Cumming, Alan (1965-) Actor, born in Aberfeldy. After several stage, TV and film appearances, he achieved an international reputation in the stage version of *Cabaret* (1998) and in such films as *Spy Kids* (2002).

Cunningham, Phil (1960-) Musician, born in Edinburgh. An accordionist, he plays and composes Scottish traditional music, being best known for his partnership with **Aly Bain**.

Currie, James (1756-1805) Doctor and biographer, born in Kirkpatrick-Fleming, Dumfriesshire. He is known as the first biographer of Robert Burns and editor of his works.

Currie, Ken (1960-) Artist, born in North Shields. He is noted for his series of murals painted for the People's Palace in Glasgow depicting the socialist history of Glasgow.

Cuthbert, St. (c.635-67) Monk and missionary, born in Lauderdale. Prior at Old Melrose and bishop of Hexham and later Lindisfarne, he travelled widely as a missionary and several miracles were attributed to him.

Cuthbertson, Sir David (1900-89) Biochemist, born in Kilmarnock. During World War II he undertook important research on the treatment of burns, later, becoming involved in improvements to animal feeding for human requirements.

D

Daiches, David (1912-2005) Scholar and literary critic, born in Sunderland, brought up in Edinburgh. His works of criticism include *Burns the Poet* (1950). Other works include *Two Worlds* (1956) about of his upbringing in Edinburgh.

Dale, David (1739-1806) Industrialist and philanthropist, born in Stewarton, Ayrshire. In 1785 he set up cotton mills in New Lanark where he introduced new methods of employee welfare. He was the father-in-law of **Robert Owen**.

Dalglish, Kenny (1951-) Football player, born in Glasgow. He played for Celtic before transferring to Liverpool for a record fee

(1977). He was capped for Scotland 102 times before going into football management.

Dalrymple, Alexander (1737-1808) Hydrographer, born in New Hailes, Midlothian. He created a series of pioneering admiralty charts and was the first official hydrographer to the Royal Navy (1795).

Dalrymple, Hugh (1700-53) Agricultural improver. He invented hollow-pipe drainage which allowed the drying-out of water-logged land. This technique was able to bring large areas of land into agricultural use.

Dalyell, Tam (1932-) Politician, born in The Binns, West Lothian. He became a Labour MP in 1962, frequently opposing official party policy, particularly Scottish Devolution. In 2001 he became the oldest serving MP.

Darling, Sir Frank Fraser (1903-79) Naturalist and ecologist, born in Edinburgh.

He worked in animal genetics before becoming an important figure in the conservation movement. He wrote *The Natural History of the Highlands and Islands* (1947).

David I (c.1080-1153) King of Scotland. During his reign he consolidated the power of the monarch, introduced Scottish coinage, reformed the Scottish church and established a common law of Scotland.

Deacon Blue Rock group formed in Glasgow in 1985 by singer and songwriter Ricky Ross (1957-). Their first album *Raintown* (1987) was a UK chart success.

Demarco, Richard (1930-) Artist, born in Edinburgh. He became a leading promoter of modern artists, both Scottish and foreign. He co-founded the Traverse Theatre in 1963 and became director of the Richard Demarco Gallery (1966).

Deness, Mike (1940-) Cricketer, born in Bellshill. He played for Scotland before joining Kent in 1962. He then captained England's cricket team very successfully and scored over 25,000 runs.

Dewar, Donald Campbell (1937-2000) Labour politician, born in Glasgow. Secretary of State for Scotland (1997-99), he was a strong advocate of devolution and became the first First Minister of the Scottish Parliament (1999) until his untimely death.

Dewar, James (1842-1923) Physicist and chemist, born in Kincardine, Fife. He devised the structure for benzene called the Dewar formula, achieved the liquefaction of hydrogen and invented the vacuum flask.

Dickson, Barbara (1947-) Singer, born in Dunfermline. Originally a folk singer, she appeared in Willy Russell's musical

John, Paul, George, Ringo and Bert (1973) before becoming a pop star, achieving early success with *Answer Me* (1976).

Dinnie, Donald (1837-1916) Highland Games Champion, born near Aboyne, Aberdeenshire. He excelled at all the Highland Games events, such as caber throwing and hammer throwing, as well as weight-lifting and wrestling.

Dolly the sheep (1997-2003) Named after country singer Dolly Parton, she was the first mammal to be successfully cloned, at Roslin Institute near Edinburgh, but developed severe arthritis and had to be put down in 2003.

Donald, Ian (1910-1987) Obstetrician, born in Paisley. Professor of Midwifery at Glasgow University, he was a pioneer of ultrasound diagnosis and originated the pregnancy scanner.

Donaldson, Sir David (1916-96) Artist, born near in Chryston, near Glasgow.

One of the best-known twentieth-century portrait painters, he painted the portrait of Her Majesty the Queen in 1966.

Donaldson, Margaret (1926-) Psychologist, born in Paisley. Her work and publications, such as *A Study of Children's Thinking* (1963) and *Children's Minds* (1978), have had a great influence on the psychology of children and education.

Donegan, Lonnie (1931-2002) Musician, born in Glasgow. He played a prominent part in the skiffle movement of the 1950s. His hits included *Rock Island Line* and *Cumberland Gap*.

Douglas, Bill (1934-91) Actor, writer and film director, born near Edinburgh. He is noted for his film trilogy *My Childhood* (1972), *My Ain Folk* (1973) and *My Way Home* (1977), based on his poverty-stricken childhood.

Douglas, David (1798-1834) Botanist and traveller. He went on three expeditions to North America to collect plants, trees and shrubs to bring to Britain. Among the trees was the Douglas fir.

Douglas, Gavin (c.1474-1522) Poet and bishop, born in Tantallon Castle. He is noted for his translation of Virgil's *Aeneid*, the first complete one in any form of English and an important work in the Scots language.

Dowding, Hugh Caswell Tremenheere, Lord (1882-1970) Air Force chief, born in Moffat. He organized the air defence of Great Britain (1936-40), the German air force being defeated at the Battle of Britain (1940).

Drummond, William of Hawthornden (1882-1970) Poet and author, born in Hawthornden, near Edinburgh. Among his works are *Tears on the Death of Moeliades*, about Henry, eldest son of James VI (1613).

Duffy, Carol Ann (1955-) Poet and playwright, born in Glasgow. Her poetry collections include *Standing Female Nude* (1985), *Mean Time* (1993), for which she won the Whitbread Prize, and *The World's Wife* (1999).

Dunbar, William (c.1460-c.1514) Poet, probably born in East Lothian. One of the great poets of the age, he wrote *The Thrissil and the Rois* in celebration of the marriage of James IV and Margaret Tudor in 1503.

Duncan, John (1866-1945) Artist, born in Dundee. Many of his paintings depicted subjects from Celtic mythology and he was one of the most important exponents of the Celtic Revival movement of c.1900.

Duncan, Reverend Henry (1774-1846) Minister, born near Dumfries. He set up a savings bank (1810) with a view to helping his poorer parishioners. This marked the start of the savings bank movement.

Dunlop, John Boyd (1840-1921) Inventor, born in Dreghorn Ayrshire. He patented an inflated tyre (1888) and is credited with inventing the pneumatic tyre although one was patented in 1845 by **Robert William Thomson**.

Dunn, Douglas Eaglesham (1942-) Poet, born in Inchinnan, Renfrewshire. His first collection of poems *Terry Street* (1969) was widely acclaimed and *Elegies* (1985) written on the death of his first wife, won the Whitbread Prize.

Dunnet, Dorothy (née **Halliday**) (1923-2001) Novelist and artist, born in Dunfermline. She exhibited at the Royal Academy, but she is best known as the writer of two series of popular historical romances.

E

Eardley, Joan (1921-63) Artist, born in Sussex, but moved to Glasgow. She is noted for her paintings of poor children from Glasgow tenements and later for her landscapes and seascapes of the north east coast of Scotland.

Easton, Sheena (originally **Sheena Orr**) (1959-) Singer, born in Bellshill. She is noted for the theme song to the James Bond film *For Your Eyes Only* (1981).

Elder, John (1824-69) Marine engineer and shipbuilder, born in Glasgow. He patented in 1853 the compound marine engine, which had a significant effect on the efficiency of steamships.

Elgin, Thomas Bruce, 7th Earl of (1766-1841) Diplomat. When Ambassador to the Ottoman Empire (1799-1803), he transported the Parthenon Frieze, later known as the Elgin Marbles, from Athens to Britain. They are housed in the British Museum.

Elliot, Walter (1888-1958) Politician, born in Lanark. As Minster for Health (1938-40) he introduced free milk for children and organized the evacuation of children from London.

Erskine, John (1695-1768) Advocate. Professor of Scots law at Edinburgh University, he wrote *Institutes of the Law of Scotland* (1773), a standard classic of Scots law still in use.

Ewart, Charles (1769-1846) Soldier. A sergeant in the Scots Greys, he captured the standard of the French 45th regiment at the Battle of Waterloo and was promoted to ensign. There is a statue of him on the Esplanade of Edinburgh Castle.

Ewing, Winnie (Winifred Margaret)
(1929-) Politician, born in Glasgow. Scottish Nationalist MP for Hamilton (1967-70) and Moray and Nairn (1974-79), she became an MEP (1975), being known as Madame Ecosse, and an MSP (1999).

F

Faed, Thomas (1826-1900) Artist, born in Gatehouse-of-Fleet. Considered to be one of the most important Scottish artists of the Victorian period, he is noted for his paintings of scenes from Scottish life.

Fairlie, Andrew (1963-) Chef, born in Perth. He established his award-winning restaurant at the exclusive Gleneagles Hotel in 2001 and was Scottish Chef of the Year (2002).

Ferguson, Adam (1723-1816) Philosopher, born in Logierait, Perthshire. A supporter of the Common Sense School of philosophy, his *Essay on the History of Civil Society* (1767) influenced political thought and help to lay the foundations of sociology.

Ferguson, Sir Alex (1941-) Football manager, born in Glasgow. An extremely successful manager of Aberdeen, he achieved even more success as manager of Manchester United. In 1999 the team won the English premiership, the FA Cup and the Champions League.

Ferguson, Patrick (1744-80) Soldier, born in Edinburgh. In 1776 he invented a breech-loading rifle which could be loaded and fired more rapidly, being able to fire seven shots a minute.

Fergusson, J.D. (1874-61) Artist. One of the Scottish Colourists, he is known for his World War I paintings of naval dockyards and his portraits of the female nude.

Fergusson, Robert (1750-74) Poet, born in Edinburgh. He wrote poems in English and Scots, his best-known work being

Auld Reekie (1773) about Edinburgh. He was a major influence on Robert Burns.

Finlay, Ian Hamilton (1925-) Poet and artist, born in Nassau, Bahamas. He is noted for his fusion of art, sculpture, poetry and landscape gardening which he demonstrates at his home Little Sparta in the Pentland Hills near Edinburgh.

Fisher, Gregor (1953-) Actor, born in Glasgow. A stage, television and film actor, he is best known for his comic portrayal of Rab C Nesbitt in the TV series of the name.

Fisher, Archie (1939-) Folk singer and broadcaster, born in Glasgow. First as part of a duo with his brother Ray and then solo, he contributed greatly to the revival of Scottish folk music.

Fleming, Sir Alexander (1881-1955) Bacteriologist, born in Ayrshire. In 1928 he discovered the antibacterial powers of penicillin, but it was Howard Florey and Ernst Chain who perfected a method of producing the drug in the 1940s.

Fleming, Robert (1845-1933) Financier, born in Dundee. Described as the father of the investment trust, he set up the Scottish American Investment Trust in 1873. He is the grandfather of Ian Fleming, creator of James Bond.

Fleming, Tom (1927-) Actor, director and commentator, born in Edinburgh. As a director he is noted for his revival of **David Lyndsay**'s *Ane Satyre of the Thrie Estatis* (1984, 1991). As a commentator he specialized in royal and state events.

Flint, Sir William Russell (1880-1970) Artist, born in Edinburgh. Originally an illustrator, he is best known for his detailed watercolour studies of the semi-nude female form.

Forbes, George (1849-1936) Physicist and engineer, born in Edinburgh. With **James Young** he improved the method of measuring the velocity of light. In 1880 he forecast the existence of Pluto.

Forbes, James David (1809-68) Physicist and glaciologist, born in Edinburgh. His scientific research contributed to the concept of a continuous radiation spectrum. He discovered that glacier velocity is directly related to the steepness of the slope.

Forbes-Mackay, Alistair (1878-1914) Naval surgeon. As part of Shackleton's expedition he reached the Magnetic South Pole in 1909, three years before Amundsen and Scott reached the Geographic South Pole.

Fordun, John of (c.1320-c.1384) Chronicler. He wrote *Chronica Genus Scotorum*, a patriotic history of the Scots from their beginnings until 1153 which became important source material.

Forman, Denis (1917-) Film director, born near Dumfries. Chairman of Granada Television (1974-87) and Deputy Chairman of the Granada Group (1884-1990), he is particularly remembered for his association with *The Jewel in the Crown* (1984).

Forsyth, Reverend Alexander (1769-1848) Inventor, born in Belhelvie, Aberdeenshire. In 1807 he patented a detonating mechanism for firearms which resulted in the British army adopting the percussion cap.

Forsyth, Bill (1946-) Film director, born in Glasgow. He became famous with *Gregory's Girl* (1981) and *Local Hero*

(1983), about the impact of the oil industry on a remote Scottish community.

Forte, Charles, Baron Forte of Ripley (1908-) Hotel magnate, born in Italy. He began his catering career in the family ice cream business. He formed the Trusthouse Forte merger in 1970 and was chief executive (1971-78), becoming chairman in 1982.

Foulis, Robert (1707-76) Printer and bookseller, born in Glasgow. His firm produced high-quality editions of the classics and he founded an Academy of Fine Arts in Glasgow in the 1750s.

Fraser, Hugh, Lord Allander (1903-66) Businessman, born in Glasgow. Under his management the family's Glasgow draper's store gradually expanded to become the substantial House of Fraser firm and a major force in the Scottish retail trade.

Fraser, Captain Simon, of Knockie (1773-1852) Fiddler and music-collector born in Invernesshire. His collection *The Airs and Melodies Peculiar to the Highlands of Scotland and the Isles* (1816) is important to Gaelic music.

Frazer, Sir James G. (1854-1941) Social anthropologist and classicist, born in Glasgow. He is known as the author of *The Golden Bough*.

Fulton, Rikki (1924-2004) Actor, born in Glasgow. He was a stage, film and television performer, best remembered for his television comedy sketches in *Scotch and Wry* (1978) and especially for his portrayal of the Reverend Jolly.

Fyffe, Will (1885-1947) Comedian and singer, born in Dundee. He performed in music halls and later on stage and in films. He is particularly remembered for his song *I Belong to Glasgow*.

G

Gallacher, Bernard (1949-) Golfer, born in Bathgate. He was the youngest member of the European Ryder Cup team in 1969 and captained the team from 1991 to 1995.

Gallacher, Willie (1881-1965) Politician, born in Paisley. He was a leading member of the militant trade unionist movement during the World War I unrest on the Clyde and was a founding member of the British Communist Party.

Galloway, George (1954-) Labour MP, born in Dundee. He was ousted from the Labour Party (2003) over his criticism of the Iraq invasion. Forming the party Respect, he won the seat of Bethnal and Bow from Labour (2005).

Galloway, Janice (1956-) Author, born in Saltcoats. Her first novel was *The Trick is to Keep Breathing* (1989). Her later work includes *Clara* (2002) about the life of Clara Schumann.

Galt, John (1779-1839) Author, born in Irvine. A prolific writer, particularly about life in small towns, he is best known for *The Annals of the Parish* (1821), about the life of a parish minister.

Garden, Mary (1874-1967) Opera singer, born in Aberdeen. Debussy created the role of Melisande for her in his opera *Pelleas et Melisande* (1902). In 1910 she began a 20-year association with Chicago Grand Opera.

Garioch, Robert (pseudonym of **Robert Garioch Sutherland**) (1909-81) Poet. He wrote in the Scots language in various forms, his poetry being influenced by that of **Robert Fergusson**.

Ged, William (1609-1749) Printer and goldsmith, born in Edinburgh. He invented the printing process of stereotyping and also the 'Lost Wax' process of metal casting, used for reproducing delicate designs in jewellery.

Geddes, Jennie (c.1600-60) Edinburgh vegetable-seller who, according to tradition, started a riot by throwing her stool at the pulpit in St Giles Cathedral as a protest against the reading of the New Book of Common Prayer.

Geddes, Sir Patrick (1854-1932) Town planner and botanist, born in Ballater. Regarded as the father of town planning, he is known for his extensive programme of redevelopment of Edinburgh's Old Town.

Gibbon, Lewis Grassic (pen name of **James Leslie Mitchell**) (1901-35) Writer, born in Auchterless, Aberdeenshire. He is noted for his trilogy *A Scots Quair,* comprising *Sunset Song, Cloud Howe* and *Grey Granite*.

Gibson, Alexander (1926-95) Conductor, born in Motherwell. In 1959 he became the first Scottish principal conductor and artistic director of the Scottish National Orchestra and he played a major role in establishing Scottish Opera in 1962.

Gillies, Anne Lorne (1944-) Singer. Originally a traditional Gaelic singer, she underwent a classical training and greatly extended her repertoire. She has been associated with Scottish Opera and the Scottish National Orchestra.

Gillies, Sir William George (1898-1973) Artist, born in Haddington. He is noted for his watercolours of the Scottish landscape, many of which he painted directly from nature.

Glasgow Boys The name given to a group of late 19th-century Scottish artists whose conception of art was based on natural, realistic subject matter rather than on the sentimental themes of Victorian painting.

Glennie, Evelyn (1965-) Musician, born in Aberdeen. Deaf since childhood, she became an outstanding international percussion player and many leading composers have written works specially for her.

Gloag, Anne (1942-) Entrepreneur, born in Perth. With her brother **Brian Souter** she set up the bus company Stagecoach which became an international transport concern and made her one of Scotland's wealthiest women.

Gordon, Hannah (1941-) Actor, born in Edinburgh. She is best known for her television roles, as in the popular drama series

Upstairs, Downstairs (1971-75). Her stage appearances include *Shirley Valentine* (1989).

Gordon, Harry (1893-1954) Entertainer, born in Aberdeen. He performed as the Laird of Inversnecky, the fictitious village whose inhabitants provided many character sketches and much humour. He had a successful pantomime partnership with **Will Fyffe**.

Gordon, Sir John Watson (1788-1864) Artist, born in Edinburgh. After the death of **Henry Raeburn** he was acknowledged to be Scotland's most important portrait painter.

Gow, Neil (1727-1807) Musician, born in Inver near Dunkeld. Scotland's most famous fiddle-player, he composed a wide range of strathspeys, reels, jigs and laments. His son **Nathaniel** continued his work.

Graham, Kenneth (1859-1932) Children's author, born in Edinburgh. His best-known work, *The Wind in the Willows* (1908), was originally written in the form of letters to his son Alastair.

Graham, Thomas (1805-69) Chemist, born in Glasgow. He formulated Graham's Law on the diffusion of gases and discovered the properties of colloids and their separation by dialysis.

Gray, Alasdair (1934-) Writer and artist, born in Glasgow. Originally a painter of portraits and murals, he is best-known as a novelist, particularly for his acclaimed novel *Lanark* (1982).

Gray, Cardinal Gordon Joseph (1910-93) Roman Catholic clergyman, born in Edinburgh. Ordained a priest in 1935, he was made a cardinal in 1969, the first such appointment in Scottish history, apart from exiled clergyman living in Rome.

Gregory, James (1638-75) Mathematician, born in Drumoak, Aberdeenshire. In 1661 he invented the Gregorian reflecting telescope. He introduced the term 'infinite series' to the language.

Grierson, John (1892-1972) Film producer, born near Doune. He pioneered British and Canadian documentary films, first making his reputation with *The Drifters* (1929), a film about North Sea herring fishing.

Grieve, John (1924-2003) Actor and entertainer, born in Glasgow. He is principally remembered for his role of MacPhail, the gloomy marine engineer in *The Vital Spark*, the 1960s TV comedy series.

Grimond, Jo (1913-93) Politician, born in St Andrews. Liberal MP for Orkney and Shetland (1950-83), he was leader of the Liberal

Party (1956-67) during which time Liberal representation in parliament was doubled.

Gunn, Neil M. (1891-1973) Writer, born in Dunbeath, Caithness. His interest in Highland history and society is reflected in his novels which include *Butcher's Broom* (1934), about the Highland Clearances, *Highland River* (1937) and *The Silver Darlings* (1941).

Guthrie, Sir James (1859-1930) Artist, born in Greenock. One of the **Glasgow Boys**, he showed in his early work the naturalism which the group favoured. Later he became a well-known portrait painter.

Guthrie, Thomas (1803-73) Minister, born in Brechin. Much concerned with the welfare of destitute children, he founded the Ragged Schools (1847) which gave free education to poor children.

H

Haddow, Sir Alexander (1907-76) Pathologist, born in Broxburn, West Lothian. He carried out pioneering work in the chemical treatment of cancer.

Hailes, Sir David Dalrymple, Lord (1726-92) Judge and historian, born in Edinburgh. He is noted for his chronological work *The Annals of Scotland from the Accession of Malcolm Canmore to the Accession of the House of Stuart* (1776).

Haldane, John (1860-1936) Physiologist, born in Edinburgh. The developer of the Haldane gas analysis apparatus, he carried out important research on the role of carbon monoxide in accidents and deaths in the mining industry.

Haldane, Richard (1856-1928) Lawyer and politician. Secretary of State for War (1905-12), he reorganized the army, established the Territorial Army and laid plans for the mobilization of Britain in 1914.

Hamilton, Gavin (1723-98) Artist and art dealer, born in Lanark. Originally a portrait painter, he became interested in antiquity both as a painter and as an art collector and influenced the development of Neoclassicism.

Hamilton, Patrick (1504-28) Martyr, born near Glasgow. A Lutheran, he was burned as a heretic at St Andrews. His death did much to extend the Reformation in Scotland.

Hamilton, Thomas (1784-1858) Architect, born in Edinburgh. An exponent of the Greek Revival movement, he designed George IV Bridge, the Royal High

School (1829) and the Royal College of Physicians (1846) in Edinburgh.

Hannah, John (1962-) Actor, born in East Kilbride. Film appearances include *Four Weddings and a Funeral* and *The Mummy* (1999). TV appearances include the role of Rebus in Ian Rankin's *Black and Blue* (2000).

Hardie, James Keir (1865-1915) Politician, born near Holytown, Lanarkshire. In 1892 he became the first Labour MP representing first West Ham South. He opposed Britain's involvement in World War I.

Hastings, Gavin (1962-) Rugby player, born in Edinburgh. A powerful full-back, he made his Scottish debut in 1986 with his brother Scott and played a crucial role in the Scottish team which won the 1990 Grand Slam.

Haston, Dougal (1940-77) Mountaineer, born in Currie, Midlothian. The first Briton to climb the north face of the Eiger in 1966, he took part in the first ascent of the southwest face of Mount Everest in 1975.

Heddle, Matthew Forster (1828-97) Mineralogist, born on Hoy. His extensive collection of minerals is held at the National Museum of Scotland. *Mineralogy of Scotland* (1901), published posthumously, is considered a seminal work.

Henderson, Hamish (1919-2002) Poet, songwriter and folksong collector, born in Blairgowrie. A founder of the School of Scottish Studies, established to collect and record folk material, he made a major contribution to the Scottish folk tradition.

Hendry, Stephen (1969-) Snooker player, born in Edinburgh. Having turned professional, he became the youngest World

Champion in 1990, winning the title again five times before losing it in 1997.

Henry, George (1858-1943) Artist, born in Irvine. One of the **Glasgow Boys**, his works tend to be more decorative and symbolic in quality than most of the rest. He sometimes collaborated with **E. A. Hornel**.

Henryson, Robert (c.1420-c.1500) Poet. Probably a schoolmaster in Dunfermline, he played a major role in medieval Scots poetry. His best-known work is *The Testament of Cresseid*, a sequel to Chaucer's *Troilus and Criseyde*.

Hill, David Octavius (1802-70) Artist and photographer, born in Perth. In partnership with **Robert Adamson**, he used the photographic calotype process to produce various works, including a portrait of the founders of the Free Church of Scotland (1843).

Hislop, Joseph (1887-1977) Opera singer, born in Edinburgh. He was a leading international tenor who played a wide range of roles. He later became coach to many leading opera singers.

Hogg, James (known as the **Ettrick Shepherd**) (1770-1835) Poet and writer, born in Ettrick in the Borders. He is noted for his prose work *The Private Memoirs of a Justified Sinner* (1824).

Hornel, E(dward) A(tkinson) (1864-1933) Artist, born in Australia. He moved to Scotland in childhood and, through his association with **George Henry**, became one of the **Glasgow Boys**. Later he specialized in painting children at play.

Hume, David (1711-76) Philosopher, born in Edinburgh. One of the best-known figures of the Scottish Enlightenment, he wrote *A Treatise on Human Nature* (1738-40) and had a great influence on the empiricist philosophers of the 20th century.

Hunter, Russell (1925-2004) Actor, born in Glasgow. He is best known for his one-man plays *Cocky* (1969) and *Jock* (1972) and for his role as Lonely in the TV series *Callan* (1967-72).

Hutcheson, Francis (1694-1746) Philosopher, born in County Armagh, Ireland. Professor of Moral Philosophy at Glasgow, he developed the theory of 'moral sense' which holds that moral judgements are the result of intuition rather than reasoning.

Hutton, James (1726-97) Geologist, born in Edinburgh. His theory of uniformitarianism with reference to the formation of rocks met strong opposition, but his ideas form the basis of modern geology.

I

Imlach, Hamish (1940-96) Musician and entertainer, born in Calcutta. He played a major part in the revival of the Scottish folk scene in the 1960s.

Inglis, Elsie Maud (1864-1917) Surgeon and suffragette, born in Naini Tal, India. She founded a maternity hospital in Edinburgh completely staffed by women (1901) and founded the Scottish Women's Suffragette Federation (1906).

Innes, Calum (1962-) Artist, born in Edinburgh. Known internationally for his abstract paintings, he was shortlisted for the Turner Prize in 1995.

Ireland, John (c.1440-95) Theologian and writer. He was private chaplain to James III and James IV and wrote the earliest known original work of Scots prose *The Meroure of Wisdome*.

Irvine, Andy (1951-) Rugby player, born in Edinburgh. He was noted for his speed and attacking skills and played for Scotland 51 times, becoming director of Scottish Rugby in 2005.

Isaacs, Alick (1921-67) Biologist, born in Glasgow. While researching influenza viruses he, with Jean Lindemann, isolated the substance, now known as interferon, which has proved to be therapeutic in some viral diseases and cancers.

Isaacs, Sir Jeremy (1932-) TV executive, born in Glasgow. Associated with many popular programmes such as *Panorama* and *The World at War*, he was the first Chief Executive of Channel 4 (1981-87).

Ivory, Sir James (1765-1842) Mathematician, born in Dundee. His work in applied mathematics included research into the gravitational attraction of ellipsoids and work on atmospheric refraction and the orbits of comets.

J

Jackson, Gordon (1923-90) Actor, born in Glasgow. He was noted for his television appearances, particularly in *Upstairs, Downstairs* (1970-75) and for his film roles in such films as *The Prime of Miss Jean Brodie* (1969).

James I (1406-37) King of Scots, born in Dunfermline. A capable, if ruthless, ruler he was also a poet and wrote *The King's Quair*. He was assassinated in Perth by dissident nobles.

James IV (1473-1513) King of Scots. An extremely successful ruler and a patron of the arts, he was killed, with much of his army, fighting the English at Flodden (1513), one of the great tragedies of Scottish history.

James VI (1566-1625) King of Scots, also King of England and Ireland (1603), born in Edinburgh. He is remembered internationally for his association with the Authorized Version of the Bible (1611) which he ordered.

Jamesone, George (1589-1644) Artist, born in Aberdeen. A portrait painter who trained in Edinburgh, but practised in Aberdeen, he is held to be the first major artist in the history of Scottish art.

Jamieson, John (1759-1838) Lexicographer and editor, born in Glasgow. He compiled *the Etymological Dictionary of the Scottish Language* (1808-09) and edited *The Brus* by **John Barbour** and *Wallace* by **Blind Harry**.

Jardine, Quintin (1946-) Writer, born in the west of Scotland. He is the author of a series of popular crime novels featuring Skinner, an

Edinburgh detective. These include *Skinner's Rules* (1993) and *Skinner's Ghosts* (1998).

Jardine, Sir William (1880-74) Naturalist, born in Edinburgh. A noted ornithologist, he edited *The Naturalists' Library* and wrote many of the 40 volumes himself.

Jenkins, Robin (1912-) Writer, born in Cambuslang. Several of his novels are set in foreign countries, such as Afghanistan, where he taught English. His best-known novels include *The Cone Gatherers* (1955) and *Fergus Lamont* (1979).

Johnson, James (c.1772-1811) Music publisher and engraver, born in the Ettrick Valley. He was the initiator of *The Scots Musical Museum* (1787-1803) to which Robert Burns contributed many songs.

Johnston, Calum (1891-1973) Gaelic singer, born in Barra. With his sister Annie he provided a great deal of information to song-collector **Marjorie Kennedy-Fraser**, thereby helping to preserve Gaelic musical culture.

Johnston, Sir Reginald Fleming (1874-1938) Traveller and colonial administrator. He travelled widely in China, writing about life there, and became tutor to the last emperor of China when the latter was 13.

Johnstone, Jimmy (1944-) Footballer, born in Viewpark, Lanarkshire. A Celtic player (1961-75), he was a talented wing-player known as Jinky. He was a member of the Lisbon Lions which won the European Cup in 1967.

Johnstone, William (1897-1981) Artist, born in Denholm in Roxburgh. His innovative work shows the influence of continental artists, particularly the Surrealists, and he was also a noted teacher of art.

Jones, John Paul (originally **John Paul**) (1747-92) Naval officer, born in Kirkbean. A supporter of the American Revolution, he has been called 'the father of the American Navy' and was noted for his bold raids around the British coast.

Justice, Sir James Robertson (1905-75) Actor, best known for his robust comedy roles in such films as *Doctor in the House, Whisky Galore* (1949) and *Chitty Chitty Bang Bang* (1968).

K

Kames, Henry Home, Lord (1696-1782) Philosopher and judge. A leading figure in the Scottish Enlightenment, he wrote on law, legal history, philosophy and aesthetics, his most famous work being *Elements of Criticism* 1762.

Kay, John (1742-1826) Artist, born near Dalkeith. He produced a *Series of Original Portraits and Caricature Etchings with Biographical Sketches and Anecdotes* (1837) which provides an entertaining and vivid look at Edinburgh life of the time.

Kelman, James (1946-) Novelist, born in Glasgow. He writes stark realistic novels about the poor and dispossessed and his novel *How Late It Was, How Late It Was* won the Booker Prize in 1994.

Kelvin, William Thomson, 1st Baron (1824-1907) Inventor and physicist, born in Belfast. He created the Kelvin temperature scale in 1848, carried out research on thermodynamics and hydrodynamics and invented various electrical instruments.

Kemp, Lindsay (1939-) Mime artist, dancer and director, born on Isle of Lewis. He has created several colourful ballets and has appeared in several films such as Ken Russell's *Valentino* (1977) and Derek Jarman's *Sebastian* (1975).

Kemp, Robert (1908-67) Dramatist, born in Hoy. He encouraged the broadcasting of Scots drama and wrote several plays. He adapted for stage Robert Lyndsay's *Ane Satyre of the Thrie Estatis* (1948).

Kennaway, James (1928-68) Novelist, born in Auchterarder. His first and best-known novel *Tunes of Glory* (1956) about class conflict in a Scottish regiment became a major film for which Kennaway wrote the screenplay.

Kennedy, A. L. (1965-) Writer, born in Dundee. Her short story collections include *Indelible Acts* (2002) and her novels include *So I Am Glad* (1995) and *Everything You Need* (2000).

Kennedy, Charles (1959-) Politician, born in Inverness. Elected MP for Ross, Skye and Inverness in 1983, the youngest MP at the time, he became leader of the Liberal Democrat Party in 1999.

Kennedy, Helena, Baroness Kennedy of the Shaws (1950-) Barrister, born in Glasgow. In addition to her high-profile legal career, she is a noted writer and broadcaster on such issues as women's rights.

Kennedy, Sir Ludovic (1919-) Writer and broadcaster, born in Edinburgh. Associated with several popular TV crime series such as *Your Verdict* (1962), he has written several books on miscarriage of justice, including *A Presumption of Innocence* (1974).

Kennedy-Fraser, Marjory (1857-1930) Musician. She did much to keep Gaelic music alive by making collections of Gaelic songs, published as *Songs of the Hebrides* (1909), and making recordings of some of them.

Kerr, Deborah (originally **Deborah Jane Kerr-Trimmer**) (1921-) Actress, born in Helensburgh. She moved to Hollywood after the success of *Black Narcissus* (1947) and achieved several successes including *From Here to Eternity* (1953) and *The King and I* (1956).

Kesson, Jessie (originally **Jessie Grant McDonald**) (1916-94) Novelist, born in Inverness. The experiences of her early poverty-stricken life formed the basis of her successful novel *The White Bird Passes* (1958).

Kidd, Carol (1945-) Jazz singer, born in Glasgow. An established singer since the age of 15, she achieved particular fame when she was invited to sing with Frank Sinatra at Ibrox stadium (1990).

Kidd, Dame Margaret Henderson (1900-88) Lawyer, born in Linlithgow. She was the first woman to be called to the Scottish Bar (1923) and the first woman QC in Scotland (1948).

Kinnaird, Alison (1949-) Glass artist and musician, born in Edinburgh. Her artistic work on glass has been widely exhibited in the UK and abroad. Her playing and teaching of the clarsach have helped to revive its popularity.

Knox, John (c.1531-72) Churchman, born in Haddington. A major figure in

Scottish religion for his contribution to the establishment of Protestantism as the established religion, he has been much blamed for the effects of Calvinism on Scottish society.

Knox, John (1778-1845) Artist, born in Paisley. Originally a portrait painter, he later specialized in panoramic landscapes. He helped to establish Glasgow as a centre of art.

L

Laing, Alexander Gordon (1793-1826) African explorer, born in Edinburgh. He identified the approximate location of the source of the Niger but failed to reach it. In 1826 he was the first European to reach Timbuktu.

Laing, R. D. (1927-89) Psychiatrist, born in Glasgow. He proposed that mental illness, particularly schizophrenia, should be seen as a positive experience and he controversially implied that the responsibility for the condition might lie with the patient's family.

Lang, Andrew (1844-1912) Writer, born in Selkirk. A historian, he also had a great interest in myth, being the author of *Myth,*

Ritual and Religion (1887) and *Modern Mythology* (1897). He wrote fairy stories for children.

Lauder, Sir Harry (1870-1950) Music-hall entertainer, born in Portobello. Extremely popular both at home and abroad, he did much to foster the caricature image of the Scot as a kilt-wearing, drunk, miser.

Laurie, John (1897-1980) Actor, born in Dumfries. Originally a respected stage actor, he made his film debut in 1929. He is best remembered now for his role as the gloomy Private Frazer in the TV comedy series *Dad's Army* (1968-77).

Lavery, Sir John (1856-1941) Artist, born in Belfast. He became a leading member of the Glasgow School and was greatly in demand as a society portrait painter.

Law, Andrew Bonar (1858-1923) Statesman, born in Canada. A Unionist

MP from 1900, he held various Cabinet posts. He retired as Leader of the House in 1921 but returned as Prime Minister (1922-23) after Lloyd George's resignation.

Law, Denis (1940-) Footballer. He made his international debut at the age of 18 and spent most of his career playing for Manchester United. He scored 30 goals for Scotland.

Law, John (1671-1729) Financier and gambler, born in Edinburgh. He unsuccessfully tried to persuade the Scottish parliament to adopt his plans to issue paper currency, outlined in *Money and Trade Considered* (1705).

Lawson, Charles (1794-1873) Botanist and traveller, born in Edinburgh. He introduced the Austrian Pine and the Cypress trees to Britain and the Cypress variety he introduced is called after him, *Cupressus Lawsonii*.

Lee, Jennie, Baroness Lee of Ashbridge (1904-88) Politician, born in Lochgelly. Elected MP for North Lanark at 24, she married Aneurin Bevan in 1934. Appointed the first Arts Minister in 1964, she was involved in the founding of the Open University.

Lennox, Annie (1954-) Singer, born in Aberdeen. She formed the Eurythmics with Dave Stewart, but went solo in 1992. In 2004 she won an Oscar for the song *Into the West* from the film *the Lord of The Rings*.

Leonard, Tom (1944-) Poet, born in Glasgow. He has experimented with various forms of poetic metres. The best of his early work was collected as *Intimate Voices: Writing (1965-83)*.

Leslie, Sir John (1766-1832) Physicist, born in Largo, Fife. He invented a differential thermometer, a hygrometer and a photometer and succeeded in producing ice artificially. by freezing water under an air pump.

Liddell, Eric (1902-45) Athlete and missionary, born in China of Scottish parents. He won gold and bronze medals in the 1924 Paris Olympic games, his achievements being remembered in the film *Chariots of Fire* (1981).

Lind, James (1716-94) Naval physician, born in Edinburgh. He conducted research which confirmed the importance of citrus fruits as a cure for scurvy and persuaded the Admiralty to supply lemon juice to sailors.

Linklater, Eric (1899-1974) Novelist, born in Penarth in Wales of Orcadian descent. He became famous with *Juan in America* (1931) and wrote many other novels such as *Magnus Merriman* (1934), *Private Angelo* (1946) and *The Ultimate Viking* (1955).

Lipton, Sir Thomas (1850-1931) Grocer and entrepreneur, born in Port Glasgow. He opened a grocer's shop in Glasgow (1870) the first of a chain. He revolutionized purchasing and marketing techniques in the retail grocery trade, becoming a millionaire.

Liston, Robert (1794-1847) Surgeon, born in Linlithgow. He was the first surgeon to use a general anaesthetic and he invented the Liston splint.

Littlejohn, Sir Henry Duncan (1826-1914) Doctor, born in Edinburgh. As Edinburgh's first Medical Officer of Health he did much to improve sanitation and introduced a legal requirement to give notification of occurrences of infectious diseases.

Livingstone, David (1813-73) Explorer and missionary, born in Blantyre. He discovered the Victoria Falls of the Zambesi and died while trying to discover the source of the River Nile. He was passionately opposed to the slave trade.

Logan, Jimmy (1928-2001) Entertainer, born in Glasgow. He made stage appearances in the 1930s with his parents and siblings as The Logan Family and went on to have a very successful career on stage, in pantomime, on radio and on screen.

Lorimer, Sir Robert Stodart (1864-1929) Architect, born in Edinburgh. His best-known public works include the Thistle Chapel at St Giles in Edinburgh and the National War Memorial in Edinburgh Castle.

Lorimer, William (1885-1967) Classicist, born near Dundee. He translated the New Testament from Greek into Scots. His manuscripts were revised and published after his death by his son Robert Lorimer.

Lulu (originally **Marie McDonald Lawrie**) (1948-) Singer and actor, born in Glasgow. Her first hit single was *Shout* (1964). She sang the theme song from, and acted in, the film *To Sir with Love*. She jointly won the 1969 Eurovision Song Contest.

Lyle, Sandy (1958-) Golfer, born in Shrewsbury of Scottish parents. He won the British Open Championship in 1985 and the US Masters in 1988.

Lynch, Benny (1913-46) Boxer, born in Glasgow. He won the world flyweight title in 1935 and the American title in 1937. He became an alcoholic and died of poverty at 33.

Lyndsay, Sir David, of the Mount (c.1486-1555) Poet and courtier. He is known for his morality play *Ane Satyre of the Thrie Estatis* about the bad practices of the lords, commons and clergy.

M

MacAdam, John Loudon (1756-1836) Engineer, born in Ayr. He developed macadmization in which a road is covered with small broken or crushed stones. Later, tar was added to form tarmacadam.

MacAlpin, Kenneth (d. 858) King of Picts. Traditionally credited with unifying the Picts and Scots into one kingdom, although this is no longer thought to be the case.

McAlpine, Sir Robert (1847-1934) Builder, born in Newarthill, Lanarkshire. A pioneer of the use of concrete in construction, he was known as 'Concrete Bob' and established an internationally successful construction company.

MacBeath, Jimmy (1894-1972) Singer, born in Portsoy, Banffshire. A tramp and busker, he became well-known in the 1950s as a singer, and oral source, of traditional and Border ballads.

MacCaig, Norman (1910-96) Poet, born in Edinburgh. Winner of the Queen's Medal for poetry in 1986, his many works include *Far Cry* (1943), *Rings on a Tree* (1968) and *The White Bird* (1973) and *Voice-Over* (1988).

McColgan, Liz (née **Lynch**) (1964-) Athlete, born in Dundee. She won the gold medal in the 10,00 metres in the 1986 and 1990 Commonwealth Games and the silver medal in the 1988 Olympics.

MacColl, Ewan (originally **James Miller**) (1915-89) Musician, born in Salford. Often working with Peggy Seeger, he was a pioneer of the folk-music revival, being best known for such songs as *Dirty Old Town* (1946).

MacCormick, John MacDonald (1904-61) Nationalist, born in Glasgow. A founder member and first chairman of the Scottish National Party (1934), he was instrumental in organizing the Scottish covenant (1949), signed by 2 million people.

MacCrimmon family. Established the famous MacCrimmon School of Piping in Skye. Patrick Mor (1595-1670) is regarded as one of the best composers of pibroch and Patric Og (1645-1730) as the best of the MacCrimmon players.

MacCrone, Guy (1898-1977) Born in Birkenhead. He moved to Glasgow and wrote several novels, but he is best known as the founder (with **James Bridie**) of the Citizens' Theatre in Glasgow.

MacCunn, Hamish (1868-1916)
Composer, born in Greenock. Much of his work was Scottish in character and theme and he is best known for *The Land of the Mountain and the Flood* (1887).

MacDairmid, Hugh (Christopher Murray Grieve) (1892-1978) Poet, born in Langholm. The leading figure in the Scottish Renaissance, he encouraged the regeneration of Scots as a literary language. *A Drunk Man Looks at the Thistle* (1926) is one of his best-known works.

McDermid, Val (1955-) Novelist. She has written several novels featuring private detectives Kate Brannigan and Lindsay Gordon. *The Wire in the Blood* (1997), featuring crime profiler Tony Hill, was televised.

MacDonald, Flora (1722-90) Born in south Uist. She led **Prince Charles Edward Stewart**, disguised as her maid

'Betty Burke', to safety in Skye after the failed Jacobite Rebellion of 1945.

Macdonald, George (1824-1905) Novelist, born in Huntly. He is best known for his stories for children, such as *The Princess and the Goblin* (1872), and for his allegorical *Phantasies* (1858) which influenced later writers.

MacDonald, Sir John Alexander (1815-91) Canadian statesman, born in Glasgow. He helped to bring about the confederation of Canada and in 1867 he formed the first government of the new Dominion of Canada.

MacDonald, Margo (1945-) Politician and journalist, born in Hamilton. She won Govan for the SNP in 1973. She was elected as an SNP MSP in 1999, and as an Independent MSP in 2003.

MacDonald, (James) Ramsay (1866-1937) Politician, born in Lossiemouth. Entering parliament in 1906, he became Prime Minister of the first Labour government in 1924. In 1931 he led a predominantly Conservative National government to deal with the Depression.

MacEwan, William (1827-1913) Brewer and philanthropist, born in Alloa. He established his Fountain Brewery in brewery in Edinburgh in 1856, gave substantial donations to Edinburgh and became an Edinburgh MP.

MacEwen Sir William (1848-1924) Surgeon, born in Rothesay. He extended Joseph Lister's use of antiseptics, introduced new methods in bone surgery and pioneered important work in brain tumour surgery.

MacGeechan, Ian (1946-) Rugby player, born in Leeds. He played for Scotland from 1972 until 1979 and became coach to the Scottish team. He was then appointed director of Scottish Rugby.

MacGillivray James (1856-1938) Sculptor, born in Inverurie. His major sculptures, executed in a naturalistic style, include the statue of John Knox in St Giles Cathedral and that of Robert Burns in Irvine.

MacGillivray, William (1796-1852) Ornithologist, born in Aberdeen. Known as 'father of British ornithology', he helped with the research for the prestigious *Birds of America* by John James Audubon and wrote *A History of British Birds* (1837-52).

McGinn, Matt (1928-77) Singer, born in Glasgow. He wrote and sang folk songs which were often comic, as well as being full of social comment, and had a significant effect on the Scottish folk scene.

McGonagall, William (c.1825-1902) Supposed poet, born in Edinburgh. His poems, first published in 1878, had such terrible rhymes that they were funny and had a popular following.

McGrath, John (1935-2001) Playwright, born in Birkenhead. Founder of the 7:84 theatre company, he wrote many plays based on Scottish cultural and political life, such as *The Cheviot, the Stag and the Black, Black Oil* (1973).

McGregor, Ewan (1971-) Actor, born in Crieff. His role in *Trainspotting* (1996) established him as a major British film actor and he later acquired an international reputation for his appearances in various films such *Star Wars*.

MacGregor, William York (1855-1923) Artist, born in Finnart, Dunbartonshire. A leading member of the **Glasgow Boys**, he is best known for the large and colourful still life *The Vegetable Stall* (1884).

McIlvanney, William (1936-) Novelist, born in Kilmarnock. Several of his powerful novels, such as *Docherty* (1975) depict working life in the west of Scotland. He has also written crime fiction, such as *Laidlaw* (1977).

McInnes, Hamish (1930-) Mountaineer, born in Gatehouse of Fleet. An experienced international climber, he became a leading authority on mountain rescue and was the founder and leader of the Glencoe Mountain Rescue Team (1960-94).

Macintosh, Charles (1766-1843) Chemist, born in Glasgow. He produced the first waterproof cloth by bonding two pieces of cloth together with dissolved India rubber (1818) and gave his name to the mackintosh raincoat.

MacIntyre, Alasdair (1929-) Philosopher, born in Glasgow. A philosopher with a considerable international reputation, he wrote the trilogy *After Virtue* (1981),

Whose Justice? What Rationality? (1986) and *Three Versions of Moral Enquiry.*

Mackay, Fulton (1927-87) Actor, born in Paisley. He acted on stage (especially the Glasgow Citizens' Theatre), and film and TV, being best remembered for his role as the prison warder in the 1970s TV series *Porridge*.

McKellar, Kenneth (1927-) Born in Paisley. Although he had a wide repertoire, including opera and popular ballads, he is best known for his recordings of traditional Scots songs, including those of Robert Burns.

Mackendrick, Alexander (1912-93) Film director, born in Boston of Scottish parents. He directed the comedy *Whisky Galore* (1948) at Ealing studios and went on to make further comedies, such as *The Ladykillers* (1955) there.

Mackenzie, Sir Alexander (1764-1820) Explorer, born in Stornoway. In 1789 he discovered the Mackenzie River (named after him) in Canada. He was the first European to cross the Rocky Mountains to the Pacific Ocean (1792-93).

Mackenzie, Alexander (1822-92) Canadian politician, born in Logierait, Perthshire. Elected to the Canadian parliament in 1861, he became leader of the Liberal Party (1873) and Canada's second Prime Minister (1874-78).

Mackenzie, Sir Compton (1883-1972) Writer, born in West Hartlepool. He settled in Barra (1928). He wrote such works as *Sinister Street* (1913) as well as novels of Scottish life such as *Whisky Galore* (1947).

Mackintosh, Charles Rennie (1868-1928) Architect, artist and designer, born in Glasgow. He was the most prominent exponent of Art Nouveau in Scotland, adapting it to suit the

Scottish style. His architectural achievements include the Glasgow School of Art.

Maclaurin, Colin (1698-1746) Mathematician, born in Kilmodan, Argyll. He played an important role in the Scottish Enlightenment, and wrote *Treatise on Fluxions* (1742), giving a systematic account of Newton's approach to calculus.

Maclean, Alistair (1922-87) Novelist, born in Glasgow. He was one of the world's most successful writers of thrillers, including *The Guns of Navarone* (1957), many of his books being made into successful films.

Maclean, Sir Fitzroy (1911-96) Diplomat and writer. His books, such as *Eastern Approaches* (1949), drew on his diplomatic and military adventures and he is said to be the inspiration for James Bond.

Maclean, John (1879-1923) Political worker, born in Glasgow. He founded the Scottish Labour College to educate workers. He set up the Scottish Workers' Party and was imprisoned several times for incitement to strike and sedition.

Maclean, Sorley (1911-96) Gaelic poet, born in Raasay. He did much to regenerate the Gaelic literary language and tradition. His collections of poems include *Reothairt is Contraigh* (1977) (*Spring Tide and Neap Tide*).

MacLeod, Ally (1934-2004) Football player and manager, born in Glasgow. He managed the Scottish team which qualified for the final stages of the 1978 World Cup in Argentina and was blamed for their failure.

Macleod, George, Lord Macleod of Fiunary (1895-1991) Churchman, writer and broadcaster born in Glasgow. He founded the

Iona community (1938). A noted left-winger, he was a strong opponent of nuclear weapons.

Macleod, John James Rickard (1876-1935) Physiologist, born in Cluny, Fife. With Frederick Banting and Charles Best, he discovered insulin, used to treat diabetes, and received the Nobel Prize for physiology and medicine (1923).

Maclure, William (1763-1840) Geologist, born in Ayr. He wrote the first geological account of America in *Observations on the Geology of the United States* (1817) and challenged the view that all primitive rocks were sedimentary in origin.

Macmillan, James (1959-) Composer and conductor, born in Kilwinning. One of the most prominent composers of his time, his varied works include

The Confession of Isobel Gowdie (1990) and the opera *Ines de Castro* (1996).

Macmillan, Sir Kenneth (1929-92) Ballet dancer and choreographer, born in Dunfermline. Originally a dancer with Sadler's Wells Theatre Ballet, he became principal choreographer with the Royal Ballet. His works include *Isadora* (1981) and *The Judas Tree* (1992).

MacMillan, Kirkpatrick (1813-78) Blacksmith, born in Thornhill, Dumfriesshire. He is thought to have invented the first primitive bicycle, although he never patented the invention.

MacMillan, Roddy (1923-78) Actor and playwright, born in Glasgow. He made regular stage appearances, and wrote several plays, but is best remembered for his role of Para Handy in the TV series *The Vital Spark*.

McNeill, Billy (1940-) Footballer and manager, born in Bellshill, Lanarkshire. He contributed greatly to Celtic's success (1965-1975), including the European Cup in Lisbon (1967) and was manager in 1987, when Celtic won the Cup and League.

McRae, Colin (1968-) Rally driver, born in Lanark. In 1991 he won the British title, winning it several times subsequently. In 1995 he became the first British driver to win the World Rally Championship.

MacRae, (John) Duncan (1905-67) Actor, born in Glasgow. His stage repertoire ranged from classics to comedy. His film appearances included *Whisky Galore* (1948) and he was noted for his comic recitations such as *The Wee Cock Sparrow.*

MacTaggart, Sir William (1835-1910) Artist, born in Kintyre. Sometimes called the 'Scottish Impressionist', he became the most outstanding landscape artist of his time. His works are known for their bold colour and dramatic lighting.

Magnusson, Magnus (1929-) Broadcaster and writer, born in Reykjavik. Known for his involvement in such TV programmes as *Chronicles* (1866-80), he is best known as the quizmaster of the long-running TV programme *Mastermind* (1972-97).

Malcolm III (Malcolm Canmore) (c.1031-93) King of Scotland. He defeated Macbeth and became king in 1057. He was an effective king, but probably one of his most important acts was to marry St. Margaret.

Margaret, St. (c.1046-1093) Queen of Scotland, born in Hungary, although an English princess. She married Malcolm III and was a refining influence on Scottish cultural and religious life. She was canonized in 1251.

Martin, Rhona (1966-) Curler, born in Irvine. She skipped the British women's team which won the gold medal at the 2002 Winter Olympics at Salt Lake City.

Mary Queen of Scots (1542-87) Born in Linlithgow. One of the great romantic and tragic, if ill-advised, figures of Scottish history, she was imprisoned and forced by her nobles to abdicate, before escaping to England, where Elizabeth I imprisoned her for 19 years before ordering her execution.

Maxton, James (1885-1946) Politician, born in Glasgow. One of the Red Clydesiders and a staunch pacifist, he was imprisoned for encouraging shipyard workers to strike during World War I. He was chairman of the Independent Labour Party.

Maxwell, Gavin (1914-69) Writer, born in Wigtonshire. His most famous work is *A Ring of Bright Water* (1962), an account of his life with his pet otters in a cottage near Glenelg.

Maxwell, James Clerk (1831-79) Physicist, born in Edinburgh. Regarded as one of the world's greatest theoretical physicists, he is noted for his work on electromagnetism. His work paved the way for that of Einstein.

Maxwell, John (1905-62) Artist, born in Dalbeattie. His paintings are noted for their dream-like fantastical quality, but they are relatively few in number since the artist revised and repainted much of his work.

Meikle, Andrew (1719-1811) Inventor, born near Dunbar. He made improvements to the design of windmills, but is best known for his invention of the first effective threshing machine which he patented in 1788.

Melville, Andrew (1545-c.1622) Theologian, born in Baldowie, Angus. He preached against absolute authority in the church and advocated a presbyterial form of Church government, often being regarded as the founder of Scottish Presbyterianism.

Melville, Arthur (1855-1904) Artist, born in Angus. One of the **Glasgow Boys**, he is best known for the paintings which he created on expeditions to Spain and the Middle East.

Menzies, John (1852-1935) Bookseller and newsagent, born in Edinburgh. He extended his father's Edinburgh business substantially, establishing bookstalls in all major towns and at railway stations, this being the start of a major chain.

Mill, James (1773-1836) Philosopher and economist, born near Montrose. The father of John Stuart Mill, a friend of Jeremy Bentham, and an advocate of utilitarianism. He wrote *Analysis of the Phenomenon of the Human Mind* (1829).

Miller, Hugh (1802-56) Writer and geologist, born in Cromarty. His early career as a stonemason led to his interest in geology and he wrote a series of geological articles, later collected in *The Old Red Sandstone* (1841).

Miller, Patrick (1731-1815) Inventor, born in Glasgow. He pioneered the steamboat and designed one powered by an engine made by William Symington, launching it in 1788 on a loch near Dalswinton.

Miller, William (1810-72) Poet, born in Glasgow. He published a collection of poems in 1863, but he also wrote poems about children and childhood, being remembered for *Wee Willie Winkie*.

Milroy, Jack (James Cruden) (1915-2001) Entertainer, born in Glasgow. A performer of music-hall style entertainment, he formed a popular act with **Rikki Fulton** in which they dressed up as Glasgow 'teddy boys' Francie and Josie.

Mina, Denise (1966-) Writer, born in Glasgow. she taught criminology before taking up crime writing. She is the author of the trilogy *Garnethill* (1998), *Exile* (2000) and *Resolution* (2002).

Mitchell, Sir Thomas Livingstone (1792-1855) Explorer, born in Craigend, Stirlingshire. He was Surveyor General of New South Wales, Australia in 1828 and made four major expeditions to explore eastern and tropical Australia.

Mitchison, Naomi (1897-1999) Writer, born in Edinburgh. A keen traveller and the author of 70 books, her interest in other countries influenced her novels, *The Conquered* (1923), *Cloud Cuckoo Land* (1925) and *Black Sparta* (1928) evoking Greece and Sparta.

Mollison, James (1905-59) Aviator, born in Glasgow. He made various record-breaking solo flights, including Australia to England (1931). With his wife Amy Johnson he made the first Atlantic flight to the USA (1933).

Montgomerie, Colin (1963-) Golfer, born in Glasgow. He was a member of the successful European Ryder Cup team in 2002 and 2004 and finished second to Tiger Woods in the 2005 British Open.

Moore, Sir John (1761-1809) Soldier, born in Glasgow. He served in several parts of the world, including the Peninsular Wars. Victorious at Corunna, he was killed, his burial being immortalized in a poem by Charles Wolfe.

Morgan, Edwin (1920-) Poet, translator and critic, born in Glasgow. His collections of poems include *The Second life* (1968) and *A Love of Life* (2003). *Rite of Passage* (1976) is a collection of translations.

Morrocco, Alberto (1917-98) Artist, born in Aberdeen. Noted for his vivid landscapes and still lifes, he was also a successful portrait painter and painted the Queen Mother.

Morris, Tom (1821-1908) Golfer, born in St Andrews. Originally a maker of golf balls and a greenkeeper, he became a professional golfer and won the British Championship belt four times between 1861 and 1866.

Morris, Tom (1851-75) Golfer, born in St Andrews. The son of **Tom Morris** *(above)* and known as 'Young Tom', he won the

British Championship belt outright (1870), having won it three times in succession.

Muir, Edwin (1887-1959) Poet and translator, born in Deerness, Orkney. His collections of poetry include *The Voyage* (1946) and *The Labyrinth* (1949). With his wife **Willa Muir** he translated Kafka and other contemporary European writers.

Muir, John (1838-1914) Naturalist, born in Dunbar. He emigrated to America and developed an interest in natural history. The leader of a campaign to establish Yosemite National Park (1890), he was a pioneer of environmentalism and ecology.

Munro, Sir Hugh Thomas (1856-1919) Mountaineer, born in London. He published his *Tables of Heights over 3000 Feet* in the first issue of the Scottish Mountaineering Journal (1891), such mountains being called Munros.

Munro, Neil (1864-1930) Novelist, born in Inveraray. His works include historical Highland novels, such as *The New Road* (1914), but he is popularly remembered for his humorous tales about a Clyde puffer, collected as *Para Handy and Other Tales* (1931).

Murchison, Sir Roderick (1792-1871) Geologist, born in Tarradale. He established the Silurian System (1835) and (with Adam Sedgwick) the Devonian System. The Ugandan Murchison Falls and the Australian Murchison River are named for him.

Murdock, William (1754-1839) Engineer, born in Lugar, Ayrshire. Responsible for several innovations in the mining industry in Cornwall, he is best known as a pioneer of coal gas lighting.

Murray, Chic (1919-85) Entertainer, born in Greenock. Best known as a comedian, both with his wife Maidie Dickson and as a solo act, he also appeared in films, such as *Gregory's Girl* (1981).

Murray, Lord George (c.1700-60) Soldier. One of **Charles Edward Stewart**'s generals, he won victories at Prestonpans and Falkirk and fought bravely at Culloden, despite having being opposed to the battle.

Murray, Sir James (1837-1915) Philologist and lexicographer, born in Denholm. He began editing *The New English Dictionary,* later called *The Oxford English Dictionary*, in 1879, it being finished at Oxford after his death in 1928.

Murray, John (1745-93) Publisher, born in Edinburgh. He established a family publishing company of the name in London (1768) which was subsequently run by successive generations, also called John Murray, until 2002.

Murray-Mooney, Yvonne (née **Murray**) (1964-) Athlete, born in Edinburgh. She won the gold medal in the 3,000 metres at the European Championships (1990) and won gold in the 10,000 metres at the 1994 Commonwealth Games (1994).

Musgrave, Thea (1928-) Composer, born in Edinburgh. Much of her early work such, as *Scottish Dance Suite* (1959), was inspired by Scotland and its culture, but her later work was more varied and more abstract.

Myllar, Andrew Bookseller and printer. With Walter Chapman, a wealthy merchant, he set up Scotland's first printing press in the Cowgate in Edinburgh.

N

Nairn, Nick (1959-) Chef and restauranteur, born in Stirling. Since 1996 he has done much to inspire the popular interest in food and cooking with his regular television appearances on programmes such as *Ready, Steady, Cook.*

Nairne, Lady Carolina (née **Oliphant**) (1766-1845) Born in Gask, Perthshire. She wrote Scots songs, including *The Auld Hoose* and *The Rowan Tree,* to traditional tunes under the pseudonym Mrs Bogan of Bogan.

Napier, David (1790-1869) Marine engineer. He built the boiler for **Henry Bell**'s steamship *Comet.* He invented the surface condenser which became a standard feature of steamship propulsion.

Napier, Sir John of Merchiston (1550-1617) Mathematician and inventor, born in Edinburgh. He invented logarithms and devised a calculating machine using a set of rods known as *Napier's Bones*.

Napier, Robert (1791-1876) Shipbuilder and engineer, born in Dumbarton. He built the engines for the first four Cunard steamships and built the earliest ironclad warships. The reputation of Clyde shipbuilding was largely founded on his work.

Nardini, Daniela (1968-) Actor, born in Largs. She gained a Bafta for her TV role as Anna in *This Life* (1996) and appeared in several further TV dramas such as *Sirens* (2002).

Nasmyth, Alexander (1758-1840) Artist, born in Edinburgh. An assistant to **Allan Ramsay**, he set up as a portrait painter and painted the best-known image of Robert Burns before turning to landscape painting.

Nasmyth, James (1808-90) Engineer, born in Edinburgh. He was a pioneer in the design and building of steam-powered tools, such as the steam hammer, a planing machine and a steam pile-driver.

Neill, A. S. (1883-1973) Educator, born in Kingsmuir, Tayside. A believer in non-authoritarian, child-centred education, he started a co-educational progressive school, called Summerhill School, in Leiston, Suffolk (1927).

Neill, Bud (1911-70) Cartoonist, born in Glasgow. He was the creator of *Lobey Doser*, the popular, long-running strip cartoon which looked at Glasgow life in a Wild West setting.

Neilson, James Beaumont (1792-1865) Engineer, born in Shettleston, Glasgow. In

1828 he invented the hot-blast system of iron production which reduced the amount of coal needed and greatly improved efficiency.

Nelson, Thomas (1780-1861) Publisher, born in Throsk, near Stirling. He founded a publishing firm in Edinburgh. The firm published the works of **John Buchan**, but specialized in educational books.

Nessie The popular pet name for the Loch Ness Monster. Although almost certainly legendary, the monster is one of Scotland's main attractions and has been the subject of many searches.

Nicol, James (1810-79) Geologist, born in Traquair, near Peebles. He began a survey of Scotland and published *A Guide to the Geology of Scotland* (1844).

Nicolson, Alexander (1827-93) Gaelic scholar, born in Skye. A prolific writer in both Gaelic and English, he helped to revise the Gaelic Bible and published *A Collection of Gaelic Proverbs and Familiar Phrases* (1881).

Ninian, St. (died c.432) Bishop of Whithorn in Galloway. Bede claims that Ninian converted the Southern Picts, although authenticated information is limited. His grave at Whithorn became a place of pilgrimage.

O

Ogilby, John (1600-76) Map-maker and printer, born in Edinburgh. His most important publications are the maps of Africa (1670), America (1671) and Asia (1673).

Ogilvie, John (1733-1813) Poet, born in Aberdeen. Dr Johnson's reply to his praise of Scotland's 'many noble wild prospects' was 'the noblest prospect a Scotchman ever sees is the high road to England'.

Ogilvie, St. John (c.1579-1615) Martyr and saint, born in Banff. Hanged for his defence of the spiritual supremacy of the Pope, he was beatified in 1927 and canonized in 1976.

Oliphant, Margaret (1828-97) Novelist, born in Wallyford. A prolific writer, she is best remembered for her series of novels known as *The Chronicles of Carlingford* (1863-76) which earned her the title of the 'female Trollope'.

Orchardson, Sir William Quiller (1832-1910) Artist, born in Edinburgh. One of the most successful Scottish artists of his period, he painted social and historical situations. Among his best-known work is *Mariage de Convenance* (1884).

Orr, Robin (1909-) Composer, born in Brechin. His work includes three symphonies, choral works, chamber music and the opera *Hermiston* (1975). He co-founded the Scottish Opera (1962).

Oswald, James (c.1711-96) Composer and violinist, born in the Stirling area. His musical works combined Scots and baroque Italian elements and his violin techniques influenced Scottish fiddlers.

Owen, Robert (1771-1858) Social reformer, born in Wales. He bought cotton mills at New Lanark from **David Dale** and there he established a model cooperative community with improved housing and working conditions. He founded similar, but unsuccessful, communities elsewhere.

P

Paollozi, Sir Eduardo (1924-2005)
Artist, born in Leith. A pioneer of British Pop Art, he became noted for his large-scale metal sculptures such as *The City of the Circle and the Square* (1963).

Park, Mungo (1771-1806) Explorer, born near Selkirk. In 1795 he led an expedition to chart the course of the Niger and was drowned during another expedition to find its source.

Paterson, Bill (1945-) Actor, born in Glasgow. He worked with the theatre group 7:84 before embarking on a film and TV career, playing roles in *The Killing Fields* (1984) and *The Crow Road* (1996).

Paterson, James (1770-1806) Born in Musselburgh. He developed the modern process by which fishing nets were made by machine.

Paterson, William (1658-1719) Financier, born in Tynwald in Dumfrieshire. He proposed the establishment of the Bank of England and became a director on its foundation in 1694. He invested, and lost, heavily in the Darien scheme.

Paton, Sir Joseph Noel (1821-1901) Artist, born in Dunfermline. He painted large and detailed historical and mythological scenes, in particular *The Quarrel of Oberon and Titania*.

Peploe, Samuel John (1871-1935) Artist, born in Edinburgh. Influenced by Post-Impressionism and Fauve art in Paris, he became a leading member of the Scottish Colourists.

Philipson, Sir Robin (1916-92) Artist, born in Broughton-in Furness, Cumbria.

A major figure in the Edinburgh art establishment, he became known in the 1950s for his paintings of cockfights, but later painted a diverse range of subjects.

Pillans, James (1778-1864) Teacher and lecturer. He advocated compulsory education and invented the blackboard and coloured chalks, using them to teach geography.

Pinkerton, Allan (1819-84) Detective, born in Glasgow. In 1952 he set up a private detective agency in Chicago and was involved in the American federal investigation network, foiling an assassination attempt on Abraham Lincoln.

Pitcairne, Archibald (1652-1713) Doctor and writer, born in Edinburgh. A leading figure in the early Scottish Enlightenment, he was one of the founders of the Royal College of Physicians.

Playfair, John (1748-1819) Mathematician, geologist. He wrote *Illustration of the*

Huttonian Theory of the Earth (1802), a major geological work, which promotes and explains the work of **James Hutton**.

Playfair, Lyon, 1st Baron Playfair (1819-98) Scientist and politician, born in Chunar, India. He served on government committees on such issues as public health, the Irish potato famine and the Great Exhibition of 1851.

Playfair, William Henry (1789-1857) Architect, born in London. He designed many of Edinburgh's outstanding buildings in a Greek-revival style, including the Royal Scottish Academy and the National Gallery of Scotland.

Pont, Timothy (c.1565-1614) Map-maker. He carried out an extensive survey of Scotland. His maps were later revised and published in the atlas prepared by the Dutchman Jan Blaeu (d.1673).

Purdie, Thomas (1843-1916) Organic chemist born in Biggar. He pioneered research into the molecular structures of carbon compounds and was Professor of Chemistry at St Andrews University.

Q

Quarrier, William (1829-1903)
Philanthropist, born in Greenock. He provided residential care for orphans where children were looked after in small family groups. He also provided services for discharged prisoners and homeless people.

Queensberry, Sir John Sholto Douglas, 8th Marquis of (1844-1900) Nobleman. He gave his name to the rules of boxing, although they were actually drawn up by John Chambers and he simply gave them his seal of approval.

R

Rae, John (1813-93) Explorer, born near Stromness, Orkney. He made several exploratory expeditions to the Arctic and was the first person to bring back definite news about the likely fate of Franklin's exhibition.

Raeburn, Henry (1756-1823) Artist, born near Edinburgh. He specialized in portrait painting and painted some the leading members of Scottish society, such as Walter Scott, David Hume and James Boswell.

Ramsay, Allan (1686-1758) Poet, born in Leadhills, Lanarkshire. His best-known work is *The Gentle Shepherd: A Pastoral Comedy* (1725). He set up a circulating library (1725), thought to have been the first in Britain.

Ramsay, Allan (1713-84) Artist, born in Edinburgh. He settled in London in 1762 and was appointed portrait painter to George III. He painted several famous people, such as David Hume and Jean-Jacques Rousseau.

Ramsay, William (1852-1916) Chemist, born in Glasgow. He discovered argon, isolated helium and found neon, krypton and xenon. He was awarded the Nobel Prize for chemistry in 1904.

Randolph, Sir Thomas, 1st Earl of Moray (d.1332) Soldier and statesman. A nephew of **Robert the Bruce**, he recaptured Edinburgh Castle from the English (1314) and was a commander at Bannockburn. He became Guardian of the Kingdom in 1329.

Rankin, Ian (1960-) Writer, born in Cardenden, Fife. A prolific and award-winning author, his popular crime novels are set against an Edinburgh background and feature Inspector Rebus who first appeared in *Knots and Crosses* (1987).

Rankine, William McQuorn (1820-72) Scientist and engineer, born in Edinburgh. He did much to shape the science of thermodynamics. His publications on shipbuilding, applied mechanics and steam engines became standard textbooks.

Redpath, Anne (1895-1965) Artist, born in Galashiels. Known originally for her still life paintings, she later painted other subjects, including church interiors. She became the first woman member of the Royal Scottish Academy (1952).

Redpath, Jean (1937-) Singer, born in Edinburgh. An internationally-known singer of Scottish folk and traditional songs, she has spent considerable time in America. She is known for her interpretation of the songs of Burns.

Reid, Jimmy (1932-) Trade unionist, born in Glasgow. As shop steward of Upper Clyde Shipbuilders he came to prominence in 1971 during the work-in. A Labour candidate in the 1979 election, he later became a journalist.

Reid, John (1655-1723) Horticulturist, born in West Lothian. He is credited with writing the first gardening book in Scotland, *The Scots Gard'ner* (1683).

Reid, Thomas (1710-96) Philosopher, born in Kincardineshire. He opposed the views of **David Hume** and was a leader of the Commonsense School of Philosophy, writing *Inquiry into the Human Mind on the Principles of Commonsense* (1764).

Reith, John, 1st Baron Reith of Stonehaven (1889-1971) Born in Stonehaven. He was the first general manager of the BBC in 1922 and director general (1927-38). In 1948 the BBC Reith lectures were instituted in honour of him.

Rennie, John (1761-1821) Civil engineer, born in East Lothian. He built various important bridges, such as Waterloo Bridge, and planned London Bridge. He also built docks and harbours including the London docks.

Richardson, Sir John (1787-1865) Explorer, born in Dumfries. A member of various Arctic expeditions, he is remembered for his accurate surveys of the Canadian Arctic coast and for his contributions to ichthyology.

Robert I (Robert the Bruce) (1274-1329) King of Scots from 1306 after killing his rival John Comyn. His military successes against the English culminated in Bannockburn (1314). He secured English recognition of Scottish independence and his right to be king.

Robertson, George, Lord Robertson of Ellen (1946-) Politician, born Port Ellen, Islay. Elected MP for Hamilton in 1978, he became Secretary of State for Defence in 1997 and was Secretary General of NATO (1999-2003).

Robertson, Jeannie (1908-75) Folk singer, born in Aberdeen. A member of the travelling people, she was discovered by **Hamish Henderson** in 1953. She had a great influence on the folk music revival.

Robertson, William (1721-93) Historian, born in Midlothian. An important figure in the Scottish Enlightenment, he wrote the *History of Scotland (1542-1603)* which was greatly acclaimed.

Rob Roy (nickname of **Robert MacGregor**) (1671-1734) Scottish outlaw. He conducted a guerrilla campaign against the Duke of Montrose after the seizure of his lands and enjoyed the patronage of the Duke of Argyll. His exploits were greatly romanticized by Walter Scott.

Rochead, John Thomas (1814-78) Architect, born in Edinburgh. He is best known as the architect of the Wallace monument in Stirling.

Ross, Sir James (1800-62) Explorer, born in London. He led an Antarctic expedition (1839-43), discovering Victoria Land and the volcano Mt. Erebus. He gave his name to Ross Island and Ross Sea.

Ross, Sir John (1777-1856) Explorer, born in Wigtownshire. He conducted surveys in the White Sea and the Arctic, led an expedition (1818) in search of the Northwest Passage and discovered the Gulf of Bothnia.

Ross, William (1762-c.1791) Gaelic poet, born in Skye. He is considered to be one of the greatest writers of Gaelic love poetry.

Rowling, J(oanne) K(athleen) (1965-) Author, born in Chipping Sodbury, Gloucestershire. She moved to Edinburgh and has become famous and wealthy as the author of a series of very popular children's books featuring Harry Potter, boy wizard.

Roy, William (1726-90) Military surveyor, born in Carlisle. In 1747 he began a survey of Scotland. His maps provide a detailed cartographic record of much of Scotland, especially the Highlands.

Ruddiman, Thomas (1674-1757) Publisher and librarian, born in Boyndie, Banffshire. He published the works of **Allan Ramsay** as well as his own *Rudiments of the Latin Tongue* (1714).

Runciman, Alexander (1736-85) and **John** (1744-68) Artists, born in Edinburgh. Alexander's most important work was a series of murals in Penicuik House (destroyed 1899). John's remarkable talent is shown in *King Lear of the Storm* (1767).

Runrig Band Founded by brothers Rory and Calum MacDonald in 1973 which combines modern Rock and Celtic influences and has gained an international reputation. In 2003 they celebrated their 30th anniversary with a concert at Stirling Castle.

S

Salmond, Alex (1954-) Politician, born in Linlithgow. Elected SNP MP for Banff and Buchan in 1987, he was leader of the SNP (1990-2000) and was re-elected to the leadership in 2004.

Schaw, William of Sauchie (1550-1602) Architect. He was responsible for the building and rebuilding of several public buildings for the return of James VI, including Dunfermline Palace and Stirling Castle.

Scott, Francis George (1880-1958) Composer, born in Hawick. He set many of Hugh MacDiarmid's early poems to music, later publishing *Scottish Lyrics Set to Music* (1922-39), including those of **William Dunbar** and **Robert Burns**.

Scott, Tom (1918-95) Poet, born in Glasgow. He wrote primarily in Scots, translating some of the works of François Villon, the early French poet, and writing a biographical narrative poem, *Brand the Builder* (1975).

Scott, Sir Walter (1771-1832) Novelist and poet, born in Edinburgh. After writing epic ballads, such as *Marmion* (1808), he became a prolific writer of popular historical novels, such as *Waverley* (1814), *The Heart of Midlothian* (1818) and *Ivanhoe* (1820).

Scott, Willie (1897-1989) Singer, born in Canobie. A shepherd with a wide repertoire of Border Ballads and songs, he was popular at folk festivals and influenced younger singers.

Selkirk, Alexander (or **Selcraig**) (1676-1721) Sailor, born in Lower Largo. The inspiration for Daniel Defoe's *Robinson*

Crusoe, he spent four years alone on the uninhabited island of Juan Fernandez.

Shand, Sir James (Jimmy) (1908-2000) Accordionist, born in East Wemyss, Fife. He achieved popularity with his appearances on the TV series *The White Heather Club* and went on to have a successful international career.

Shankly, Bill (1913-81) Football player and manager, born in Glenbuck, Ayrshire. A successful international player, his greatest achievement was his managership of Liverpool (1959-74), which achieved home and international success under him.

Sharp, Alan (1934-) Novelist and scriptwriter, born in Alyth. His wrote a successful first novel *A Gree Tree in Gedde* (1965), but turned to scriptwriting, his films including *The Hired Hand* (1971) and *Rob Roy* (1995).

Shearer, Moira (1926-) Ballet dancer, born in Dunfermline. She joined Sadler's Wells in 1942 and danced a number of major roles, but she is best known for her part in the ballet film *Red Shoes* (1948).

Shepherd-Barron, John (1925) Inventor. He worked for De La Rue Instruments in the 1960s and invented the Automated Teller Machine (ATM), the first one being installed in London in 1967.

Sibbald, Sir Robert (1641-1722) Naturalist and physician, born in Edinburgh. He established the first botanical garden in Edinburgh in 1970 and founded the Royal College of Physicians.

Sim, Alastair (1900-76) Actor, born in Edinburgh. He is best known for his wide range of film characters, ranging from the sinister, including *Green for Danger* (1946), to the comic, including *The Belles of St Trinians* (1954).

Simple Minds Glasgow rock group, including singer Jim Kerr and guitarist Charlie Burchill, which became one of the most prominent stadium acts of the 1980s, also achieving success in America.

Simpson, Sir James Young (1811-70) Obstetrician, born in Bathgate. He was a pioneer in the use of anaesthetics, particularly chloroform. He also pioneered improved obstetric techniques and reformed hospital practices.

Sinclair, Sir John, of Ulbster (1754-1835) Agricultural reformer, born in Thurso. Responsible for the compilation of the first Statistical Account of Scotland (1791-99), he undertook research into crop rotation and sheep farming.

Skene, William (1809-92) Historian, born in Knoidart. A solicitor, he researched Scottish historical documents in his spare time and is best remembered for *Celtic Scotland* (1876-80).

Skinner, James Scott (1843-1927) Fiddler and composer, born in Banchory. Known as the 'Strathspey King', he was a talented Scots and classical player. Among his many compositions is *The Bonnie Lass o' Bon Accord*.

Slessor, Mary (1848-1915) Missionary, born in Aberdeen. She became a missionary in Nigeria, providing healthcare and education to the local people, who called her 'Great Mother', and stamping out cruel practices, while respecting local customs.

Small, James (1730-93) Agricultural inventor. Originally a joiner in Berwickshire, he invented the curved cast-iron plough which was much more effective than the original wooden ones.

Smellie, William (1740-95) Writer, born in Edinburgh. With two friends, he produced the first edition of the *Encyclopaedia Britannica* (1768-71), writing much of it himself. He printed the first edition of Burns's poems.

Smiles, Samuel (1812-1904) Writer and social reformer, born in Haddington. He wrote several works designed to improve people, the best-known being *Self-Help* (1859), a book of short lives of great men.

Smith, Adam (1723-90) Economist and philosopher, born in Kirkcaldy. He is best known for his *Inquiry into the Nature and Causes of the Wealth of Nations* (1776) in which he discusses such issues as the division of labour.

Smith, Sir Alexander McCall (1948-) Writer, born in Zimbabwe (then southern Rhodesia). He is the writer of the popular series of novels featuring the detective Mma

Ramotswe and set in Botswana, including *The No1 Ladies' Detective Agency* (1998).

Smith, Ali (Alison) (1961-) Writer, born in Inverness. She gained recognition with *Free Love and Other Stories* (1995). Her novels include *Hotel World* (2001) which was shortlisted for the Booker Prize.

Smith, Elaine (1958-) Actor and comedian, born in Baillieston, Glasgow. A stage, television and film actor, she is probably best known for her role as the wife in the TV comedy series *Rab C Nesbitt*.

Smith, George (1824-1901) Publisher, born in Elgin. He extended the London publishing business Smith, Elder & Co, started by his father, publishing the Brownings, Thackeray and Charlotte Brontë, and began *The Dictionary of National Biography*.

Smith, Ian Crichton (1928-98) Poet and novelist, born in Lewis. He wrote poetry in both Gaelic and English. Of his novels the best known is *Consider the Lilies* (1968), a powerful novel about the Highland Clearances.

Smith, James (1789-1850) Agricultural reformer, born in Deanston, near Doune, Perthshire. He developed a system of sub-soil drainage which had a revolutionary effect on agriculture.

Smith, John (1724-1814) Bookseller, born in Strathblane, Stirlingshire. He established the firm of **John Smith and Son** in Glasgow, which was to become very successful, and started Glasgow's first circulating library.

Smith, John (1938-94) Politician, born in Dalmally. Elected MP for Lanarkshire North in 1970 and Monklands East from 1983, he was leader of the Labour Party after Neil Kinnock's resignation (1992) until his untimely death.

Smith, Robert Angus (1817-84) Environmental chemist, born in Glasgow. He was the first to identify what is now known as acid rain and campaigned for the introduction of smokeless fuels when working in Manchester.

Smith, Sir Sydney Goodsir (1915-75) Poet, born in Wellington, New Zealand. He established a reputation as a writer in Scots, publishing such poems as *Under the Eildon Tree* (1948), and wrote the play *Wallace*.

Smollett, Tobias (1721-71) Novelist, born in Vale of Leven. His first novel was *Roderick Random* (1748), but he is best known for *Humphrey Clinker* (1771), an epistolary novel about a trip round Britain.

Sole, David (1962-) Rugby player, born Aylesbury. A prop forward who captained Scotland over 20 times, he is best remembered for leading the Scottish team to victory in the Grand Slam in 1990.

Somerville, Mary (1780-1872) Mathematician and astronomer, born in Jedburgh. She wrote several works explaining comprehensibly various aspects of the science of astronomy, physics, etc. She was a strong supporter of the emancipation of women.

Soutar, William (1898-) Poet, born in Perth. Prominent in the Scottish 20th-century literary revival, he wrote much of his poetry in Scots, including *Seeds in the Wind* (1933) (for children) and *Poems in Scots* (1935).

Souter, Brian (1954-) Entrepreneur, born in Perth. With his sister **Anne Gloag** he set up the bus company Stagecoach which became an international transport concern and made him one of Scotland's wealthiest men.

Spark, Muriel (1918-) Novelist, born in Edinburgh. A prolific writer of remarkable novels, she is popularly known for *The Prime of Miss Jean Brodie* (1961), the story of a teacher with a remarkably strong influence over her pupils.

Spence, Sir Basil (1907-76) Architect, born in India of Scottish parents. One of the leading British architects of the post-war period, he designed various university buildings, including Southampton. He is best known for the new Coventry Cathedral (1951).

Stair, James Dalrymple, 1ˢᵗ Viscount (1619-95) Politician and jurist. Lord President of the Court of Session, he wrote the definitive work on Scots law *Institutions of the Law of Scotland* (1681).

Steel, Sir David (1938-) Politician, born in Kirkcaldy. Sponsor of the Abortion Reform

Bill (1966-67), and the last leader of the Liberal Party, he was an MSP (1999-2003), and the first Presiding Officer of the Scottish Parliament.

Steell, Sir John (1804-91) Sculptor, born in Aberdeen. His works include the marble statue of Sir Walter Scott on the Scott Monument in Edinburgh and the equestrian statue of the Duke of Wellington in Edinburgh.

Stein, Jock (1922-1985) Football manager, born in Burnbank, near Hamilton. Manager of Celtic when they won the European Cup in 1967, he led the team to ten League Championships, eight Scottish Cups and six League Cups.

Stevenson, Robert Louis (1850-94) Novelist, born in Edinburgh. He is perhaps best known for his first novel *Treasure Island* (1883) and for *Kidnapped* (1886). He is also remembered for the sinister *Dr Jekyll and Mr Hyde* (1886).

Stevenson, Ronald (1928-) Composer, born in Blackburn, Lancashire of Scottish parents. A prolific composer of a wide range of works, he has composed many pieces reflecting the influence of Scottish traditional music.

Stewart, Andy (Andrew) (1933-94) Comedian and singer, born in Glasgow. Best remembered for his own composition *A Scottish Soldier,* he made regular appearance in the 1960s TV series *White Heather Club* and had his own show from 1963.

Stewart, Belle (1906-97) Singer, born in Caputh, Perthshire. A traveller with a great knowledge of Scots songs and stories in the oral tradition, she became a well-known folk singer, as did several members of her family.

Stewart, Dugald (1753-1828) Philosopher, born in Edinburgh. Much influenced by the Commonsense School of Philosophy of

Thomas Reid, and a prolific author, he is best remembered for his exceptional teaching ability.

Stewart, Sir Jackie (John Young) (1939-) Racing driver, born in Dunbartonshire. He won the world title in 1969, 1971 and 1973, and became chairman of the Paul Stewart racing team in 1989.

Stewart, J.I.M. (pen name **Michael Innes**) (1906-94) Novelist, born in Edinburgh. Under his own name he wrote popular novels with an Oxford academic setting, and, under his pseudonym, detective novels featuring Inspector Appleby.

Stewart, Mary (1916-) Novelist, born in England. A writer of suspense, historical fiction and fantasy, she is best remembered for her Arthurian trilogy, *The Crystal Cave, The Hollow Hills* and *The Last Enchantment*.

Stewart, Rod (1945-) Rock singer, born in London of a Scottish father. He sang with The Faces until 1975 and as a solo artist. He is noted for such hits as *Maggie May* and *Sailing*.

Stewart, Prince Charles Edward (1720-88) Known as the Young Pretender and Bonnie Prince Charlie. One of the best-known and most romantic figures in Scottish history, he unsuccessfully tried to reclaim the Scottish throne in the second Jacobite rebellion (1745).

Stirling, James (1926-92) Architect, born in Glasgow. Noted for his work in Britain and Europe, he designed the Neue Staatsgalerie, Stuttgart (1880-84) and the Clore Gallery in the Tate Gallery in London (1987).

Stirling, Patrick (1820-95) Mechanical engineer, born in Kilmarnock. He was the most eminent of a family of locomotive engineers and developed the eight-foot single-driver express locomotive, noted for its speed and power.

Stuart, John McDouall (1815-66) Explorer, born in Dysart. He made several expeditions to the interior of Australia and crossed from the north to the south. Mount Stuart is named after him.

Syme, James (1799-1870) Surgeon, born in Edinburgh. He pioneered new surgical techniques, especially in amputation, and experimented with the reconstructive surgery we call plastic surgery today.

Symington, William (1763-1831) Inventor, born in Leadhills, Lanarkshire. He patented a steam-powered road vehicle and a similar engine for a paddle-wheel boat and in 1802 he built one of the first working steamboats.

T

Tassie, James (1735-99) Artist and modeller, born in Pollokshaws, Glasgow. He developed a special enamel composition for making portrait medallions and made cameo portraits of prominent people.

Tedder, Arthur W., Lord (1890-1967) Air Force commander, born in Glenguin, Stirlingshire. From 1940 he commanded the Middle East Air Force, later becoming General Eisenhower's deputy supreme commander. He was made Marshal of the RAF in 1945.

Telfer Jim (1940-) Rugby player and coach, born in Pathhead, Midlothian. As coach, he took the Scottish national team to the Grand Slam in 1984, a feat repeated in 1990. He became Director of Rugby in 1999.

Telford, Thomas (1757-1834) Civil engineer, born near Langholm. He built many bridges, docks and canals, including the Caledonian Canal (1803-23), the Menai Suspension Bridge and the St Katherine's Docks in London.

Tey, Josephine (pseudonym of **Elizabeth Mackintosh**) (1897-1952) Crime writer. She is best remembered for *The Daughter of Time* (1952) which investigates the alleged murder by Richard III of the little princes in the Tower of London.

Thin, James (1824-1915) Bookseller. He opened his own bookselling business in Edinburgh in 1848, becoming a friend of such authors as Robert Louis Stevenson. The business remained in the Thin family until 2002.

Thomas the Rhymer (c.1220-97) Seer and poet. His prophecies, which included the Battle of Bannockburn, were published in 1602. Legend has that he spent some time in Elfland.

Thomson, Alexander ('Greek' Thomson) (1817-1875) Architect, born in Balfour, Stirlingshire. He experimented with new techniques to form an individual style based on pure Greek, Egyptian and Indian elements. Surviving works include Moray Place, Glasgow (1859).

Thomson, D(avid) C(ouper) (1861-1954) Newspaper proprietor, born in Dundee. The firm DC Thomson, which he managed until his death, still flourishes today, publishing magazines and comics as well as the *Dundee Courier* and the *Sunday Post*.

Thomson, Derick (1921-) Poet, born in Stornoway. Collections of his poems include *Creachadh na Clarsaich*, translated as

Plundering the Harp (1982). He also wrote *An Introduction to Gaelic Poetry* (1974).

Thomson, James (1700-48) Poet, born near Kelso. He is remembered for his long poem *The Seasons* (1730) which influenced Wordsworth. His *Alfred, a Masque* (1740) contains the words of *Rule Britannia*.

Thomson, Robert William (1822-73) Inventor, born in Stonehaven. He patented the first vulcanised rubber pneumatic tyre in 1845, but it was considered too expensive. He also patented the fountain pen and a steam traction engine.

Torrance, Sam (1953-) Golfer, born in Largs. He won several international tournaments, and represented Scotland in World and Dunhill Cups. He captained the winning Ryder Cup team in 2002.

Townsend, Gregor (1973-) Rugby player, born in Edinburgh. First capped for Scotland in 1993, he established a record number of appearances for the national side.

Tranter, Nigel (1909-2000) Novelist and historian, born in Glasgow. A prolific writer, he is best known for his novels on historical themes, such as his trilogy on the life of Robert Burns and *The Wallace* (1975).

Traquair, Phoebe Anna (1852-1936) Artist, born in Dublin. A noted enameller, especially of religious subjects, she married Ramsay Traquair, head of the Natural History Museum in Edinburgh, and became a central figure in the Celtic revival movement.

U

Unna, Percy (1878-1950) Environmentalist and philanthropist, born in London. He formulated Unna's Rules, guidelines for the conservation of Scottish mountains and made generous donations to the National Trust for Scotland.

Ure, Midge (1953-) Musician, born in Cambuslang, Glasgow. A member of the band Slik, he then became a solo performer. Much involved in Band Aid (1984), he helped to organize the G8 Edinburgh charity concert in 2005.

Urquhart, Fred (1912-95) Writer, born in Edinburgh. He wrote novels such as *Time Will Knit* (1938), but is best remembered for his supernatural short stories, *Seven Ghosts in Search* (1983).

Usher, Andrew (1826-98) Whisky distiller, born in Edinburgh. He established the process of blending Scotch malt and grain whiskies and funded the building of the Usher Hall in Edinburgh.

V

Valentine, James (1815-80) Photographer and publisher. He opened a studio in Dundee and became noted for his landscape photographs. His company started making postcards in the 1890s.

Vettriano, Jack (1951-) Self-taught artist, born in Kirkcaldy. His stylized works are popular with the public, although not always with art critics. His *Singing Butler* in 2004 fetched a record price for a Scottish painting.

W

Waddell, Willie (1921-92) Football player and manager, born in Forth, Lanarkshire. He played for Rangers (1938-56), being capped for Scotland 17 times. A very successful manager for Rangers from 1969, he redeveloped Ibrox after the disaster of 1971.

Wallace, Sir William (c.1274-1305) Freedom fighter, probably born near Paisley. He defeated Edward I's army at Stirling Bridge (1297), but Edward defeated Wallace's army at Falkirk (1298). Wallace escaped but was later captured and executed (1305).

Walton, E(dward) A(rthur) (1860-1922) Artist, born in Renfrewshire. One of the most important of the **Glasgow Boys**, he is noted for his rural landscapes and scenes of village life.

Walton, George (1867-1920) Brother of **Edward Walton**, artist and designer of furniture, glass and textiles. He received commissions for the design of the Cranston tearooms in common with **Charles Rennie Mackintosh**.

Warner, Alan (1964-) Novelist, born in Oban. His first novel *Morvern Callar* (1995) was published to much acclaim. Later works include *The Sopranos* (1998) and the surreal black comedy *The Man Who Walks* (2002).

Watson, W(illiam) J(ohn) (1865-1948) Gaelic scholar, born in Easter Ross. His *History of Celtic Place-names of Scotland* (1926) remains the major work on the subject.

Watson-Watt, Sir Robert Alexander (1892-1973) Physicist, born in Brechin, Angus. He developed radar and introduced it during World War II. He was made scientific advisor to the Air Ministry in 1940.

Watt, Alison (1965-) Artist, born in Greenock. She was the winner of the National Portrait Gallery's annual portrait competition (1987). Later she became known for her studies of female nudes.

Watt, James (1736-1819) Inventor, born in Greenock. He greatly improved the steam engine by introducing a separate condenser and invented the governor as a control device. The watt, a unit of electrical energy, is named after him.

Watt, Jim (1948-2005) Boxer, born in Glasgow. In 1979 he won the WBC World Lightweight Championship, defeating Columbian Alfredo Pitalua. He successfully defended his title four times.

Weir, Judith (1954-) Composer, born in Cambridge. Her interest in folklore and theatre has had a great influence on her wide-ranging musical works which include the opera *A Night at the Chinese Opera* (1987).

Weir, Molly (1910-2004) Entertainer and writer, born in Glasgow. An excellent mimic, she came to prominence in *ITMA* in the 1940s, being recently well-known for her role in the children's TV programme *Rentaghost*.

Weir, Tom (1914-) Climber and journalist, born in Glasgow. He has climbed in the Himalayas and other parts of the world and written on environmental issues. He is noted for his TV series *Weir's Way*.

Weir, William Douglas, 1st Viscount Weir of Eastwood (1877-1959) Born in Glasgow. He became Secretary of State for War in 1918 and he was responsible for the creation of the RAF.

Wells, Alan (1952-) Athlete, born in Edinburgh. He won a gold medal in the 100 metres at the 1978 Commonwealth Games and at the 1980 Moscow Olympics, also winning the 100 metres and 200 metres at the 1982 Commonwealth Games.

Welsh, Alex (1829-82) Jazz musician, born in Edinburgh. A cornet and trumpet player, he moved to London and became an important figure in the revival of traditional jazz.

Welsh, Irvine (1958-) Novelist, born in Leith. His successful novel *Trainspotting* (1993) about the drug scene was an even more successful film (1996). He also wrote short stories called *The Acid House* (1995).

White, Kenneth (1936-) Poet and essayist, born in Glasgow. He developed the idea of geopoetics and set up the International Institute of Geopoetics in France 1989, further centres being established in other countries.

Wilkie, Sir David (1785-1841) Artist, born in Cults, Fife. He achieved great success with *The Village Politician* (1806) and is known for his genre pictures scenes, such as *Reading the Will* (1811).

Wilkie, David (1954-) Swimmer, born in Edinburgh. He won gold in the 200 metres breaststroke at the 1976 Montreal Olympics in a record time, also winning silver in the 100 metres.

Williamson, Duncan (1928-) Storyteller, born in Argyll. As a traveller, he acquired a great knowledge of oral traditional folklore and wrote several books based on this, such as *Silkies and Fairies*.

Wilson, James (1742-98) American politician, born near Ceres, Fife. He moved to Philadelphia, becoming an advocate of American independence. With James Madison he was responsible for the final draft of the American Constitution (1787).

Wilson, Jocky (1951-) Darts professional, born in Kirkcaldy. He won the World Darts Championship in 1982 and again in 1989.

Wilson, John (pen name **Christopher North**) (1785-1854) Writer. An early contributing editor to *Blackwood's Magazine*, he is known for his *Noctes Ambrosianae* (1822-35), a series of imaginary conversations set in an Edinburgh tavern.

Wilson, Thomas Brendan (1928-2001) Composer, born in Colorado, USA. Resident in Scotland for most of his life, he composed in a wide range of forms, including the opera *The Confessions of a Justified Sinner* (1976).

Wishart, George (c.1513-46) Protestant martyr, born in Angus. Charged with heresy, he went into exile, returning in 1543. He was burnt at the stake in St. Andrews on Cardinal Beaton's orders.

Witherspoon, John (1723-94) Theologian, born in Gifford. Emigrating to America in 1768, he became a representative to the Continental Congress (1776-82) and helped to frame the American declaration of independence (1776).

Wolfson, Sir Isaac (1897-1991) Businessman and philanthropist, born in Glasgow. He joined Universal Stores in 1932, becoming managing director in 1934. Having made a fortune, he established the charitable Wolfson Foundation in 1955.

Wood, Wendy (Gwendoline Meacham)
(1892-81) Scottish Nationalist political activist, born in Maidstone. Although only one quarter Scots, she was a committed founder member of the National Party of Scotland (1928) and an inspirational speaker and broadcaster.

Wright, Frances (Fanny) (1795-1852) Social reformer, born in Dundee. A wealthy heiress, she emigrated to America in 1818 and campaigned vigorously for female emancipation and the abolition of slavery.

Wright, John Michael (1617-94) Artist. He became an important portrait painter, being particularly known for his portrait of Charles II and that of Lord Mungo Murray.

Wright, Reverend Kenyon (1932-) Clergyman, born in Paisley. A missionary in India, he returned to Scotland and became General Secretary of the Scottish Churches

Council (1981-90). He played a prominent part in the Scottish Constitutional Convention.

Wylie, George (1921-) Artist, born in Glasgow. He uses a wide variety of materials in his work, some of them large-scale, unusual and dramatic. He created a full-scale floating paper boat and launched it on the Clyde (1989).

Wyntoun, Andrew (c.1355-1420) Historian. He wrote *Orygnal Cronykil of Scotland* a lengthy history, written in rhyming couplets and covering the period from the Creation to 1406.

Y

Yarrow, Sir Alfred Fernandez (1842-1932) Shipbuilder, born in London. He moved his shipbuilding business north to Scotstoun on the Clyde in 1907, establishing Yarrow's Shipyards.

Young, Douglas (1913-73) Poet and dramatist, born in Tayport, Fife. Jailed for refusing to take part in World War II because there was no independent Scottish army, he is noted for his translations into Scots of the plays of Aristophanes.

Young, James (nicknamed '**Paraffin**' **Young**) (1811-33) Industrial chemist, born in Glasgow. His experiments with paraffin production led to the development of the shale industry in Scotland in West Lothian.

Z

Zavaroni, Lena (1963-99) Singer, born in Rothesay. Noted for her huge voice, she became an international pop star and had her own television show at the age of 14.

All Crombie Jardine books are available from your High Street bookshops, Amazon, Littlehampton Book Services, or Bookpost (P.O.Box 29, Douglas, Isle of Man, IM99 1BQ. tel: 01624 677 237, email: bookshop@enterprise.net. Free postage and packing within the UK).

www.crombiejardine.com/scots

If you have any comments about who should
be in a new edition (or, indeed, who should
be taken out), please let us know by contacting
us at: greatscots@crombiejardine.com